SOUL
SELFIE

HOW TO CLICK INTO YOUR REAL SELF

T0303740

SADGURU RAMESHJI

BEL!EF

Reprint 2020

FiNGERPRINT! **BEL!EF**

An imprint of Prakash Books India Pvt. Ltd.

113/A, Darya Ganj, New Delhi-110 002,
Tel: (011) 2324 7062 – 65, Fax: (011) 2324 6975
Email: info@prakashbooks.com/sales@prakashbooks.com

facebook www.facebook.com/fingerprintpublishing
twitter www.twitter.com/FingerprintP
www.fingerprintpublishing.com

Copyright © 2019 Prakash Books India Pvt. Ltd.
Copyright Text © Sadguru Rameshji

ISBN: 978 93 8956 778 6

Processed & printed in India

This book is dedicated at the feet of
Rajendra Brahmachariji and Swamiji Sri Poornananda
without whose grace I would have never
known who I am and what the purpose of my life is.

CONTENTS

Preface

Asatoma Sadgamaya,
Tamasoma Jyotirgamaya,
Mrutyorma Amrutangamaya.

For most of my spiritual journey, these words have been my favourite prayer. It is a prayer to the Divine Mother (the Shakti), the creator of this universe: *'Oh Mother, please lead me from the unreal to the real; lead me from the darkness of ignorance to the light of knowledge; lead me from death to eternity.'*

Through this book, I hope to pay tribute to these wise words and to elucidate their true meaning.

Everyone takes selfies of their physical appearance, but nobody bothers to take selfies of their inner appearance—the inner self, the soul. While our social networking profiles always have our latest pictures, we have forgotten to update the selfie of the actual self in the database of our intellect. We rarely bother to know how we look from the inside—how smart or dull, caring or apathetic our soul is.

A soul has infinite potential, equivalent to the powers of the cosmos and universal energies. The powers of the soul include the power to create and achieve anything of its liking in the materialistic world—the power to create a favourable situation, the power to influence people, the power to be unconditionally blissful, the power to see the unseen, the power of mind over matter, the power to discard and acquire physical bodies at will, the power to leave the body and perform astral travel at will, and much more.

However, by virtue of identifying ourselves with a finite physical body we are unable to tap this infinite potential. The powers of the soul are beyond the comprehension of an unevolved mind. It is only when one evolves from an intellectual being to a soulful being that these powers become accessible.

This book reveals the secrets of living such a soulful existence independent of the physical body.

Who are we? What is our real existence? Are the body and soul two different entities? If so, how to separate them and realize our true existence? Who is our Creator? From where have we come and where are we headed? Can we choose to be happy all the time? If so, how?

This book aims to clarify and answer such existential questions through simple language, easy-to-understand examples, and various practical suggestions. It provides the master key to living life joyfully, invoking our inner potential, dispelling superstitious beliefs, and getting rid of negative emotions such as guilt, fear, anger, anxiety, expectations, attractions, and aversions.

This book also deals in great detail with our greatest fear—the fear of death. Who does not contemplate about the notion of death, or is immune to the anxiety and doubt surrounding the uncertainties of what happens after death? We keep wondering: does life exist after death? Do we continue to live even after the body dies? If so, in what form? Where? Hell? Heaven? For how long?

In answering these questions, this book helps readers live their lives fully and fearlessly, as God intended. It strips God of His remote and fearsome attitude and brings Him closer to our heart, as close as our very breath. The real meaning of devotion is revealed whereby God is freed from the confines of physical temples and worshipped in the temple of the mind, so that one can be with Him 24x7. The book also explains the Laws of Karma, clears common confusions and misconceptions about karma, and explains what one must do to escape from the endless cycle of cause-and-effect.

Through the narration of my own spiritual journey and experiences, I unravel various esoteric concepts such as the mystic powers of a yogi, kundalini shakti, the role of an enlightened master, initiation into spirituality and shaktipat by a guru, hatha yoga, dhyana, self-knowledge, the power of prana, levitation, seeing the light of the soul, playing with the soul and travelling beyond the realm of physical matter, and the guru's important role in igniting our inner divine light.

This life itself is a beautiful and rare gift from our creator, the Supreme Divine Being. It is every individual's right as well as responsibility to use this gift well by taking control of his destiny and channelizing his energies towards living a purposeful, successful, joyful and blissful life, and following a path of intellectual and spiritual evolution.

May the Divine Mother bless you all with her choicest blessings and give you all happiness, health, prosperity, purpose of life, and enlightenment.

This or That?

One day when King Janaka was taking a short nap after his lunch, he dreamt that a rival king had invaded his country and driven him out of his palace.

Janaka wandered about in the jungle, thirsty and hungry. He reached a small town where he begged for food, but no one paid him any attention. He reached a place where some people were distributing food to beggars. Each beggar had an earthen bowl to receive rice. As Janaka had no bowl, they refused to serve him any food and asked him to bring one.

He went in search of a vessel. He requested other beggars to lend him a bowl, but none would part with their own. At last he found a broken piece of a bowl and ran back but by that time all the food had been already distributed.

Janaka was dying of hunger and was so tired and exhausted that he was on the point of collapse. Seeing his pathetic condition someone took pity on him and offered him some khurchan, the burnt rice, scraped from the bottom of the cooking vessel.

Janaka took it with immense joy and was about to put some in his mouth when a large bird swooped down and tried to snatch rice from the bowl. The bowl fell to the ground spilling the leftover rice in the mud. Janaka fell unconscious.

At this point, King Janaka awoke, still crying for rice and water. He was sweating profusely and felt exhausted from the hunger, thirst, and scorching heat he had faced in the dream. It took him some time to recognize the changed scene around him. He was in his palace, in his soft bed, covered by a silken coverlet. He felt bewildered not knowing which the real dream was: was he dreaming right now about being a king or had he dreamt about being a hungry and thirsty beggar.

Unable to decide, King Janaka muttered, "Which is real, this or that?" From that time, nothing else interested him and he went on uttering only these words: "Which is real, this or that?"

The ministers thought that their king was suffering from some illness. It was announced that anyone who cured him would be richly rewarded. Great physicians and specialists began to pour in and try their luck, but no one could answer the query of King Janaka.

Finally, the great sage Ashtavakra came to the king and said, "Janaka! Neither is this real, nor that."

Hearing this King Janaka at once became alert, got out of the bed, and sat at Ashtavakra's feet, seeking more clarity. "What then is real, oh great sage?" he asked.

Ashtavakra said, "My dear king! Neither was that real nor this, but *you* are real. You, the witness to your being a beggar and the witness to your being a king, are real. You, as the soul, are real. It is the soul which is common in both the states and is the witness to both the states. Only the soul is real and everything else is unreal, oh King Janaka!"

Anything that is subject to change, decay, and destruction is temporary and is considered unreal. Anything that is imperishable, beyond decay and change, is permanent and is considered real.

Two concepts emerge from this story.

One: The physical body and the physical world are unreal as they are temporary, and subject to change, decay, and destruction.

Second: The soul is real as it is permanent, imperishable, and is not subject to change or decay.

The physical body and the physical matter in the world are made up of five elements—earth, water, fire, air, and ether—and these elements are prone to change, decay, and destruction; hence anything made up of them is considered temporary and unreal. But the soul which is the spark of *consciousness* and is beyond decay, change and destruction, is permanent and is hence considered real.

We are souls living in a physical body and operating from within. We, as souls, are the driving force behind all the movements, actions, and reactions of the physical body. We, the souls, are masters of physical matter.

Consider the analogy of the SIM card in the mobile phone. The SIM card remains the same irrespective of the mobile phone it is placed in. One may discard an old or out-dated phone, but it is the same SIM that goes into the new phone. The physical body is like the phone and the soul like the SIM card. Just as the SIM has its own identity, the soul also has its own identity. Irrespective of the mobile phone the SIM is inserted into, all the calls and messages go through the SIM. Likewise, regardless of the body the soul is placed in, all its karmas, impressions, and vibrations are carried through the soul only.

Another way of understanding this is through the example of a car. As a car is separate from its driver, the soul too is separate from the physical body. Like a car which has a body, an engine, a seat, and a steering wheel and is driven by a driver, so it is with human beings too. We too have a human body, a brain, a heart, various organs, and limbs and are driven by a driver, the soul.

Most of us, in our ignorance, consider the soul and body as a single entity and as the real one. We believe ourselves to be what we physically appear to be without realizing our separate existence as soul. This ignorance of considering physical matter as real extends to the whole world. The world is considered real and permanent even though it is subject to change, decay, and destruction.

Because we consider the physical body as real and the materialistic world as permanent we are not able to enjoy the permanent happiness that we all seek. The physical body and material objects, which are changing and decaying every moment and are moving towards destruction, cannot give permanent happiness. *Temporary matter cannot be the source of permanent happiness.* To enjoy permanent happiness, we need to shift our focus from the temporary physical matter to the permanent non-physical soul.

Our real and permanent identity is the soul. Its existence is not dependent on the physical body, as it existed before the birth of this body and will continue to exist after the death of this body too.

It's like the apple and its seed. When the apple exists, the seed exists inside it and when the apple is eaten away, the seed continues to exist outside. The seed's existence is not dependent on the existence of the apple. It exists with or without the apple. Similarly, when the body exists, the soul exists inside it and when the body dies, the soul continues to exist independent of it.

After the apple is eaten away, the seed is thrown out and that seed goes inside the soil and produces another apple tree. Similarly, when our body dies and is discarded, our soul is released into the cosmos and produces another life cycle with another body based on its karma. The soul has the potential to create endless life cycles as the seed has the potential to create endless apple trees.

As the existence of the soul is not dependent on the physical body so it is with the happiness of the soul. The soul can be happy even without a physical body or physical matter.

The happiest moment for a soul is when it is in deep sleep or when it is in deep meditation. In both these states, it is most blissful as it is disconnected from the physical body and physical world. The awareness of the physical body and anything to do with the physical world stands null and void in both these states. Whether one owns a Ferrari or has to struggle along in public transport, whether one is a beggar or the most influential person alive, whether one lives on the streets or resides in a three-acre bungalow, everything ceases to exist in these states and thus the soul enjoys bliss.

This basically proves that physical matter is an impediment to lasting happiness. Only when we are away and disconnected from physical matter do we enjoy inner bliss and happiness. In deep sleep or in deep meditation, there is no discrimination and segregation of things or people on the basis of nature, name, fame, or form, as exists in the physical world, and, since the soul is immersed in its consciousness, it experiences a blissful state.

After death too, the soul remains blissful, as it is disconnected from the physical world and the relations, aspirations, expectations, goals, and problems associated with it.

If the soul can get habituated to living constantly in such a state of deep sleep or deep meditation, even when we are awake, it can be in bliss all the time. Detachment from physical matter brings happiness and attachment to physical matter brings pain and sorrow.

For being eternally happy we have to invariably focus on our being the soul and not the physical body with which we are identified in the world. This identification with the physical body is only for the purpose of vyavahara, i.e., for operating on the physical plane, and not for getting attached to physical matter or for identification with the physical body, and definitely not for seeking happiness through the physical matter.

Being happy is the nature of the soul and to sustain its happiness, the unenlightened soul seeks it in physical matter and objects. When the soul feels happy on acquiring something of its liking or on fulfilling its desire, it is unaware that the happiness is not a quality of that object but the quality of its own self.

Happiness is the property of the soul, abundantly stocked within its inner chambers, and gets invoked through the medium of an external object. Whenever happiness gets invoked through an external object, the unenlightened soul thinks that it is the object which has given it happiness. This is where the soul gets caught in the clutches of ignorance and thus keeps seeking happiness in objects in the physical world.

Enlightened souls have been able to dispel the darkness of this ignorance and have realized the fact that happiness lies within and not outside. They have learnt to freely invoke their happiness even without the medium of an external object.

The enlightened ones have learnt to focus on the consciousness of their souls and live eternally happy lives. Even as they keep the physical body in the service of the physical world, they remain in union with their inner consciousness all the time. This was the state which Lord Krishna described in the Gita by saying: '*Yogastah kuru karmani, yogah karm kaushalam*' which means 'If you always remain in union with the Supreme Divine Being, automatically your behaviour and attitude will attain perfection.'

We too have to learn to live an enlightened life if we wish to be happy all the time. In an enlightened state, external situations and circumstances do not matter to the soul as it knows that neither its existence nor its happiness is dependent on any external object or external world. It sees everything as temporary and as a passing phase.

The constant awareness of being the soul keeps happiness intact and diversion of this awareness from soul to physical matter depletes happiness. Depletion of happiness itself is termed as sorrow and pain.

King Janaka went on to become famous for being in the state of bliss all the time. Even though he seemed to remain engrossed in the affairs of his kingdom, and enjoyed his magnificent palace and his beautiful wives, yet he remained unattached to them and uninfluenced by any favourable and unfavourable events in life. He lived an enlightened life full of bliss.

For Buddha and Mahavira, it was easy to feel bliss as they discarded all material objects and the material world. But a better and more suitable example for all of us to follow is of King Janaka. Being in the world, yet remaining detached from the worldly objects, is what we need to work on. Remaining aware of the soul as our permanent existence and performing all the duties and responsibilities on the physical plane through the physical body will lead us to the same enlightened state which King Janaka experienced.

NECTAR OF GYANA:

- Know that we are souls and not the physical body.
- The physical body is made up of five elements and is subject to change, decay, and destruction, but the soul is the spark of consciousness and is indestructible.
- Live in the world and enjoy worldly matter but without any attachment.
- Attachment gives pain and sorrow whereas detachment gives happiness.
- Keep your hands and legs in the physical world but keep your head in the forest of consciousness.
- Know that happiness is not the property of any object but is the property of the soul which can invoke it at will without the support of any external object.
- Living an enlightened life is easy as it is our nature, but living an unenlightened life is difficult as we are living against our nature.

Reservoir of Bliss

The soul is a reservoir of bliss. Peace, happiness, joy, and bliss are intrinsic to the nature of our soul. The reservoir of our soul is filled to the brim with these joyful feelings but, like the sluice gates of a dam, which when closed do not allow the reservoir water to flow to the other side, our mental state, fluctuating in response to various external stimuli, does not allow joy, bliss, and happiness to flow from our soul into our being.

Normally we are happy only when a situation is favourable, or our desire is fulfilled, or when we are appreciated, or our ego gets satisfied. In the absence of such reasons, we are generally not happy. Since our focus is mainly on the material aspect of the world, we keep stashing materialistic objects, thinking that accumulating more or more will provide for ultimate bliss. But eventually we reap only pain, misery, and sorrow. Only on switching the focus to the soul and on the hidden reservoir of bliss in it, does one realize that to satiate this quest for more and more happiness we need to keep the sluice gates of the mind open so as to allow the unhindered flow of bliss from the soul to our being.

We think happiness is hidden in objects, situations, appreciation, desire fulfilment, or ego satisfaction. But, in reality, happiness doesn't come as some kind of free attachment with any of these. It is generated within us. External factors only become the medium to invoke inner happiness. Spiritually evolved souls have been able to discern this secret and learnt to be happy and joyful without any medium or external support.

Once a rich person saw a poor sadhu sitting blissfully under a tree and asked him, "Why are you so happy? You seem to have won a lottery ticket."

The sadhu replied, "I am happy because I want to be happy. To be happy I don't need any reason or support system. Happiness is within me and is my property. I invoke it at my free will. I have learnt to be happy unconditionally."

The sadhu then looked at the rich person and said, "You don't look happy. You seem to be rich, why are you then not happy?"

The rich man said, "I don't know. I am always under stress. I feel anxious about my future and live under constant fear of losing my possessions."

The sadhu said, "That's the truth, my son. Our happiness lies within us, but it is not allowed to rise to the surface of our consciousness by our worries, fear, anxiety, enmity, hatred, and ego. Let go of these and you will be happy all the time. When you came to the world you came empty-handed and alone. Everything that you possess has been acquired here and everything will be left behind when you depart from the world."

In reality, there is nothing that we truly possess. We only believe that we do. House, land, car, business, spouse, property, and jewellery—all exist outside us and will always remain outside us. They cannot be absorbed into our being, and whatever is not inside us cannot be said to be our possession.

What we do possess are the emotions of happiness, joy, bliss, and love. We also possess mental reactions, impressions, perceptions, and karmas. These are internal to us and are our true properties and acquisitions. They remain with us irrespective of whether we are alive within a body, or without, after the death of the physical body.

Take the example of the rich man whose house caught fire while he was away on a tour. When he was informed of this and told that everything he possessed had been destroyed, he fainted from the shock of the huge loss.

After some time, when his son called and reminded him that the house had been insured and that the insurance company would reimburse the full worth of the house, he recovered and became happy.

A little later, the son called again and said that he had

just found out that the insurance policy had expired and the insurance company would therefore not honour their claim. The distressed man fainted once more.

Still later in the evening his son called yet again to inform him that there had been a miscommunication and actually it was not their house which had been destroyed in the fire, but their neighbour's. And the man became happy once again.

This is how we all become happy or sad perceiving situations as favourable or unfavourable. Such situations do not have the power to touch us physically or penetrate our being to make us happy or sad, but because of our positive or negative perception of the situation we become happy or feel sorrowful.

It's all in the mind. Happiness and sorrow are the mind's play. The concept of mind over matter actually means that mind has the power to perceive matter as per its own will. Our personal truths are what the mind perceives and believes to be true. It is not the situation that matters; what is important is our perception of it.

When we buy land, we pay some money and get it registered in our name through a sale deed. The land remains wherever it is. The seller of the land remains wherever he was, and we remain wherever we are. The land does not shift even an inch from its place. It is just through a piece of paper that we consider the land to be our property. It's a mental transaction.

If it is only a mental transaction to possess things, then what stops us from thinking that we possess the biggest property on earth, that we are the owners of the biggest business, and are the richest people on this planet? Can we not imagine that we have only given the power of attorney to others to manage our business, properties, and wealth? Can we not tell ourselves that we are so simple, modest, unfussy, and austere that, irrespective of being the richest people on earth, we live in a double-bedroom house, drive a small car, and travel in trains? That it is by choice we wear ordinary unbranded clothes, go to ordinary restaurants, and spend most of our leisure time with family?

But think for a moment: even if we were the owners of the whole earth, would we have needed something bigger to sleep in than a 3ft x 6ft bed, and could we have eaten any more than we could fit on a standard-size plate? Would we have taken up any more than two square feet of space whether we were sitting in a limousine or in a public bus? Indeed, even our grave would have been of the same size as the grave of a pauper, and inside the grave we would have been nothing more than a dead body no matter what we had been in life—kings, beggars, or saints.

When Shivaji Maharaj sent cartloads of gold coins, diamonds, and expensive jewellery to his guru, his guru returned it all, saying, "Enlightenment has made me the owner of all the three worlds, your gifts are just a speck of what I possess." This is how enlightened saints perceive the world and worldly objects and this is the reason they remain eternally happy.

For an ordinary person who is totally engrossed in worldly matters and has never been exposed to spiritual guidance, it is generally difficult to understand what one means by bliss, joy, and an inner happiness that is independent of outside situations. How can one be happy without any favourable conditions in the outside world? How can one be happy without the fulfilment of one's desires and expectations? For a person who has not experienced such a state, such gyana appears to be fanciful, untenable, or delusional.

Once, after a discourse, a person asked his spiritual master, "What is bliss? This unending pleasantness that you speak of, how does it feel? Can you explain?"

The master replied, "Bliss is a feeling which has to be experienced. It cannot be explained. However, trust that it resides in your heart. It flows from within and is the sweetest pleasure one can experience. It remains invariable and constant, irrespective of external situations and circumstances."

But the man, not trying to understand, continued to argue. "I have never experienced any such thing. I do not believe any such thing as eternal bliss or delightful joy. All of this is fake, it's all unreal!"

The master tried his best to explain through various examples and methods but the person was in no mood to give in. He was bent upon proving that the promise of undying bliss was fake propaganda, being spread by so-called saints to gain popularity.

The master abruptly picked up a brick and hit the man on his head.

Clutching his head, the man shouted in anger, "Why did you do that? Don't you know how much it hurts?"

The master asked, "Hurt, what hurt?"

The man yelled, "When we are injured, it hurts. Pain is a terrible and unpleasant sensation caused by an injury."

But the master remained unconvinced and prodded the man to explain pain.

"How do I explain pain?" the man demanded. "It has to be experienced."

"But I have never experienced pain, so I don't know what it is. There is no such thing as pain. It is all fake," said the master.

The man was furious but couldn't say anything. However, he finally understood the point the master was trying to make.

We need to experience knowledge, the gyana bestowed upon us by saints, as they have experienced it and understood its efficacy.

Knowing is not enough. Becoming is more important.

When knowledge translates into experience by practicing it in real-life situations then *knowing becomes becoming*. By not believing in higher spiritual knowledge we might miss experiencing it and never know its transformational effect on our lives. We would then never know that a reservoir of bliss exists within us.

Whenever the sluice gates of a reservoir dam are opened, the reservoir water gushes to the other side with such speed that it feels like it was waiting for just this release and liberation for ages. It makes us realize how forcefully it was held back and trapped, forced to remain stagnant against its original nature. As long as the water was dammed up, the other side remained dry, parched, and bare. The view on the side without water was dull and boring, while the view on the side with water was soothing and filled with promise, prosperity, and joy.

Our situation, too, is similar. Even though we are filled with bliss within our soul, when the mind doesn't allow that bliss to flow out we appear dry, bare, and parched. Our lives become boring, disappointing, depressive, and full of hatred, jealousy, and negativity.

With a closed and conditioned mind, we spend our entire life in delusion, uncertainty, anxiety, stress, fear, and sorrow.

Life can never be exactly the way we want it to be. There are millions and trillions of permutations and combinations for the events and situations that arise in life and they cannot always be as per our choice. But, when things do not go the way we want them to, we get distressed and depressed.

God has given us the free will to be happy even if a situation is not according to our taste. God has given us the free will to learn from failures or adversities and make them stepping stones for success.

Adversities are like the magma from volcanoes. The overflowing magma has the potential to destroy everything in its path and yet, when it cools, it is filled with nutrients, enough to grow the greenest jungle around. It has the capacity to become home to a colourful variety of flora and fauna. The end of this eruption is the beginning of something worthwhile, a beautiful environ.

But, just as we typically think of volcanic eruptions

only as catastrophic, we think of adversities as ruinous and damaging. However, like the magma or the lava, these adversities also hold equal positives to enrich us with experience and have the potential to create the best possible environment for future success and happiness. These adversities come into our lives and force us to stop and reflect about the direction of our lives. They are like reference points that we can use to adjust our behaviour for the future. They are also an opportunity to keep a check on our ego, which is the cause for most adversities in the first place. They help in releasing all the negatives within and fill us with new energy, thus paving the way for releasing our trapped potential. The end of adversity is the beginning of something new, paving the way for something better in life. Just as death is not the end of life, but the inception of a fresh life where one gets a new healthy body, discarding all the diseases and difficulties of the past life, so too do adversities help one to discard old problems and strains on relationships, and start afresh. It is just a matter of adjusting our perspective to look for the rewarding and happier side.

Adversity is inevitable, but suffering is our choice.

God has given us this free will to not expect anything from anybody and accept people and life situations as they are, but we are not using this free will to be happy. Instead, we use our free will for incorrect purposes and remain sorrowful for all the invalid reasons. Our expectations are such that no one and no situation can make us happy hence we frown at every situation in life and struggle with every person we deal with. And then, when we are left with this sadness, which is the by-product of our own inaccurate expectation, we start accumulating it within ourselves. *As per the law of focus, whatever we focus on that increases in us.* By ignorantly focusing on the negatives we increase them manifold.

Whenever we have extra money, we normally invest it in a way that promises us great returns. Similarly, we invest these stockpiled negative emotions in situations and people, not understanding that these too will come back to us with appreciated returns.

When the emotions we invest are negative, which is usually the case, we will be hit in return by shockingly amplified negatives from people and situations, which will eventually leave us holding more irritation, anger, enmity, loss, frustration, and depression than we started out with. Instead, if we invest positive emotions by making others happy, bringing smiles on their faces, and serving the needy, we will benefit with appreciated volumes of happiness, joy, and bliss in our lives. It all depends on which emotions we invest in as those are the same emotions that will come back to us in highly appreciated returns.

Think of the cosmos as an investment banker and ourselves as investors. The cosmos guarantees highest returns for our investments. Make your investments wisely so that you get back returns which give you happiness, joy, and eternal bliss.

Situations have no power in themselves; it is we who have given power to situations to influence us. People have no power over us; it is we who have given power to everyone to influence our mental state. Planets have no power over our destiny; it is we who have given unflinching powers to them by believing in astrology. Vastu has no power; it is we who have given powers to brick and cement walls to influence our fate. No black cat has the power to change our luck; it is we who have given it power through our fear when it crosses our path.

In short, we have given the remote control of our lives in the hands of objects, people, animals, and situations even though we have the power of free will to feel whatever we want to feel.

Consider the story of two friends who both invested the same amount of one million dollars in a similar type of business they both started simultaneously. At the end of one year both of them made the same profit of quarter million dollars. One friend was very happy with the profit and went on a holiday with his family, while the other friend was sad and frustrated.

When the first friend was asked why he was so happy, he said, "I expected my profits to be one hundred thousand dollars only whereas I made a profit of quarter million dollars, much more than I expected, so I am happy."

When the second friend was asked as to why he was sad when he too made the same profit as his friend, he said, "I expected a profit of half a million dollars, but I made only a quarter-million-dollar profit, hence I am feeling disappointed and frustrated."

One was happy and the other sad. This is because of

their individual expectations and perceptions. One used his free will to be happy by expecting less, while the other was sad because of his own high expectation, even though both were in exactly the same situation.

This is one of the most significant secrets of human beings' potential. Our mind is very powerful, much like nuclear fuel. And just as nuclear fuel can either be used for making a bomb for destructive purposes or for generating electricity and sustaining life, so too can the mind be turned into a tool for destruction of happiness through negativity, or for generating happiness and a force for positivity.

Think of it as two rival wolves that reside in our mind—one which feeds on negativity and the other which feeds on positivity. On their own, these wolves cannot find food. It is we who feed these wolves and the one we feed well often becomes strong and powerful while the one we feed less becomes weak. We are their masters and these wolves survive or die, become strong or weak, depending on how much we feed them.

The more we dwell on emotions such as anger, irritation, worries, and jealousy, the more nutrition the negative wolf gets, and it becomes stronger and stronger. On the other hand, when we feel more and more positive, love for every being, offer prayers and gratitude for everything, and seek forgiveness, then the positive wolf gets the most nourishing, wholesome, and nutritious feed and it grows bigger and stronger.

We are their masters and these wolves survive or die, become strong or weak, depending on how much we feed them. This is the one of the most significant secrets of human beings' potential.

Negativity of the mind is like the gravitational force of the earth. Just as the earth's gravity pulls everything down unless some force is applied to remain up in the air, the mind is pulled down by the gravity of negativity unless the force of positive thoughts, love, and compassion keeps it light and buoyant.

Just as a helicopter is able to hover above the ground because its rotor blades produce an anti-gravitational force to counter the earth's gravitational force, so too must the rotor blades of positivity be kept rotating at double the speed of negativity to prevent the mind from falling in the trap of negativity. Then, it will not have any anxiety, stress, disappointment, hatred, and fear. By keeping the rotor blade of positivity ON at all times, one will achieve and enjoy success in all aspects of life, be it business, job, relationship, or self-realization.

Another habit of the human mind is comparison. We compare ourselves with others and this generally leaves us sad and discontented, as the comparison is usually with those better than us.

Once a crow compared itself with the swan and felt disappointed with his own black colour.

He went to the swan and said, "How beautiful you are! All spic and span in white!"

The swan replied, "What is so beautiful about being white? Have you seen the parrot and his colourfully shaded feathers? That is what I call beauty!"

The crow went to the parrot and asked if his colourful feathers made him happy. The parrot said, "I am not nearly as beautiful as the peacock. He is the most beautiful bird with the most vivid variety of colours, which no other bird has!"

"Where can I see such a peacock?" enquired the crow.

The parrot said, "You can see him in the zoo."

When the crow saw the peacock in the zoo he was spellbound by his beauty. He went to the peacock and said, "You are the most beautiful bird in this world and you must be really happy."

However, the peacock said, "I am not at all happy. I think the crow must be the happiest bird in the whole universe as nobody cages a crow and it can fly wherever it wants to fly."

Even when we are happy and have all the freedom to do anything we want, we compare ourselves to others, whom we perceive to be more fortunate, and end up feeling discontented. We never realize that every being has its own set of problems in life. While the problems may vary in nature and magnitude, but everyone has some sort of suffering.

In human beings, the suffering is more psychological than real. God has given us the power of positive thinking, but seldom do we use it for our happiness.

The virtue of comparison should not be used with others but could be used in judging our own selves, whether we are limiting ourselves to the physical self with its materialistic problems or leaping towards the unfettered soul and its boundless bliss.

NECTAR OF GYANA:

- Know that your soul is the reservoir of bliss and keep the sluice gates of your mind open for the bliss to flow.
- The obstacles to opening the sluice gates of the reservoir of bliss are: focusing on negativity instead of positivity; too many conditions, perceptions, opinions, and impressions on the mind; comparison with others, which leads to discontentment.
- Adversity in life is inevitable but suffering is our choice.
- Like the magma of a volcano, adversity too has the potential to destroy but also a bigger potential to reconstruct the most beautiful life.
- Whether you emanate negativity or positivity, know that it is your investment with the cosmos and it will be given back to you in appreciated form.
- Keep the remote control of your life with yourself and use the power of free will to be happy, instead of giving it to others and thereby giving external people, objects, and situations the power to make you unhappy, sorrowful, and depressed.
- Do not compare yourself with anyone and trust God in that He has not made any mistake in making you the way you are.
- Keep the rotor blades of positivity always ON so that your mind is always floating above the trap of negativity.

Accidental or Planned?

L ife on this planet can be understood from two diametrically opposite perspectives.

The first is to consider everything in life as accidental. Everything from the 8.4 million species that exist on the planet to the differential life of human beings is accidental. Being born rich or poor, healthy or unhealthy, male or female, is accidental and having the particular parents, spouse, children, friends, foes, and relatives we have is similarly accidental. Favourable and unfavourable situations in life are accidental. Loss and profit, joy and sorrow, pain and pleasure are accidental. *Every aspect of this life is accidental.*

The second perspective is to consider that everything in this universe has been systematically planned and happens based on some law with definite rules and regulations. *Nothing is accidental.* There are no surprises in the universe—no shocks, no jolts, nothing unexpected. Everything is chalked out in advance and perfectly planned.

We can choose to believe in either of these contrasting perspectives. It is our choice and our free will.

A question may arise at this stage: what is reality, which perspective is the absolute truth?

It is a big question and difficult to be answered. Even if it is answered one way or the other, with examples and substantiation, it is up to the individual to accept the answer or not. Then, how do we solve this mystery?

The solution lies in the words of Vedas: *'Yad bhavam, tad bhavati'* which means 'what you believe, that is true. What you believe, that happens.' Whatever you choose to believe in stands true for you. It's our choice and free will to choose what suits us and believe in it as truth. There is no reward or punishment in one belief or the other. If we believe the world to be accidental, then it is so, and if we believe the world to be perfectly planned and run by specific rules and regulations, then that is correct too.

The problem is not really about which perspective to choose, but about sticking to the belief we choose.

If we choose to believe that everything happens by accident, then we should fully believe in that. Let there be no grudge against anybody for our suffering or losses, let there be no blame or negativity against anybody for whatever wrong happens to us. Let us not be disappointed when things do not go as per our wishes. After all, everything is accidental, and we have no control over accidents. Know that there is no rule or law working for favourable or unfavourable, fortunate or unfortunate events in our lives and no one is for or against us.

From this perspective, there cannot, and should not, be any complaint against or comparison with anyone. For whatever they are and whatever we are is accidental. It is as accidental as some places receiving bountiful rains while others suffering through terrible drought, or earthquakes and tsunamis occurring in some parts of the world even as other parts live in peace and prosperity.

We just have to believe in prakriti (nature). Nature doesn't operate based on individual will or intellect. It works based on its own permutations and combinations of the various elements and dimensions which constitute it, and operates under laws that are beyond our comprehension and control.

Whatever happens, happens accidentally.

Those who believe in this perspective should always remain at peace, be uncomplaining and happy, and have total acceptance of life situations, favourable or unfavourable. One cannot do anything about any situation whatsoever.

However, it is not only difficult, but almost impossible, to be like this. It is not easy to completely and unconditionally accept whatever life throws at us, especially in the face of difficulties and hardships. The mind does not accept anything at face value. It is in the nature of the mind to hunt for logic, meaning, or explanation in every situation, every action, and every reaction.

Now we are left with the second perspective of accepting life as perfectly planned, in perfect harmony, governed by unbiased laws, rules, and regulations and controlled by some supreme entity. What we choose to call that supreme entity is our choice, for the name or form we associate with this entity is immaterial and does not change the governing laws of this perspective. What is important is the recognition and acceptance of this entity's existence.

Let us understand through logical reasoning why nothing in the world is accidental. There is a reason behind every happening, though we may not always be aware of it. The laws that govern the various situations and circumstances arising in our lives are the Laws of Karma. Everything that happens in our lives is the result of previously performed karmas. Nothing happens accidentally. There are no unexpected happenings, situations; everything is pre-planned and predetermined including what we sometimes call 'coincidences'.

Coincidences too do not happen accidently but are created logically.

A child is born in a rich family in a five-star hospital and at the same time another child is born in a poor family on the footpath. What can be the cause for such different starts in life? Neither of the new-borns have had the time to do anything good or bad. Why is it then that with their very first breath on earth one child is already blessed with every luxury in life while the other is deprived of even basic amenities?

Why is one child born healthy and another child with

physical or mental disabilities? Why is one child born in a family that showers him with much love, care, education, and the best practices of upbringing, while another child is born in a family that neglects him, or that is incapable of providing for his food, education, health, and shelter?

There has to be some sound reason behind such stark differences. Not only does our very birth seem a matter of chance, but throughout our life's journey we encounter numerous people and situations that bring us happiness or pain, cause profit or loss, give us guidance or lead us astray, help or hinder, for no apparent reason. Try as we might, we are unable to find a valid cause or justification for such experiences. There are times when good fate seems to be running towards us and there are times when suddenly good fate seems to be shunning us. All of a sudden, without any perceptible reason, everything—our decisions, relationships, financial situation—seems to work in our favour. And there are times when opposite too happens, when whatever we do seems to lead to disaster.

Such an unexplained and incomprehensible state of affairs in our lives can only be seen as the result of our past karmas. *Karma is the action and situation is the reaction.* This game of action and reaction is the Laws of Karma. Whatever we are today and whatever situations we encounter in our lives is the result of our past karmas.

The Laws of Karma decides when, how, where, and in what form we get the result of our past karmas. It is present and working at all times, albeit behind the scenes, and is not controlled by any super being in a physical form.

Past karmas, which have not yet initiated their effects, keep modifying based on our new karmas, hence life situations are unpredictable.

Any prediction of the future based on astrology, palmistry, numerology, tarot card reading, vastu or any such method is totally fake, fraudulent, and bogus. When the potential effect of past karmas is continually modified based on our new karmas in the present through our mental, physical, and emotional actions and reactions, how then can anyone predict our future based on the planetary position at the time of our birth, the lines on our palms, or the name given to us when we were born. Right from our birth to the present moment, we would have performed thousands and thousands of new karmas, even as we face the effects of our old karmas, and these new karmas would have modified the uninitiated effects of our old karmas enough to produce new results altogether.

Say, for example, that you have decided to cook rice and vegetables. You cut the vegetables and keep the salt, spices, and rice ready. But before you start cooking, you happen to see a cookery show on TV on how to make the famous Indian biryani. Now you decide to change the menu from rice and curry to biryani and you mix all the vegetables in the rice itself, add salt and spices and cook it as biryani. What could have been curry and rice got converted to biryani. Similarly, our karmas could have been ready to cook a situation in our lives and kept all the ingredients ready, but just before that we performed a new karma and the old karmas got modified into a new situation by the Laws of Karma and presented to us a different effect altogether.

As karmas and the laws governing them are invisible to us, it is difficult to predict what lies in the future in advance. A situation, before manifesting in the gross physical world, is in latent form and concealed in space. It is incognito, inconspicuous, unobvious, and incomprehensible. It is also ever-changing with every new action of ours.

Sometimes karmas and their results could be correlated on a one-to-one basis. We perform good, pious karmas in the present birth and we enjoy their good results soon in life. We perform bad, sinful karmas and we suffer their results too in due course, and we are able to relate these life situations to respective karmas.

However, it is not always possible to draw such correlations between karmas and their results because past-birth karmas too spill over to our present birth. Our present-life situations could be the result of karmas from a previous birth and since we do not remember our previous births we cannot correlate our life situations with our actions in a past birth. This is where we get confused. It is something like watching one episode of a TV serial. We wouldn't understand anything of that episode unless we watch earlier episodes of the same serial. There is continuity between episodes and whatever happened in the earlier episodes directly influences the happenings in the current episode. Similarly, every event in our current life is influenced by events that happened in the past during our current or previous lives. There is continuity, though it remains hidden from us as we are limited by the perceptions of our current physical existence.

In our lives we have seen good people performing pious karmas and are good to everyone and yet are struck by adversity. They incur losses, meet with accidents, fall sick, and are deceived by people. At the same time, we see bad characters performing sinful karmas, such as smuggling, theft, cheating and unethical business practices, and yet they prosper.

When we misguidedly begin to correlate good karma to bad results and bad karma to good results, we start disbelieving in the Laws of Karma. This is one of the illusory aspects of the Laws of Karma, which can also be understood as maya. Just because the effects of karma may not be seen within the span of a single lifetime, it does not mean that bad karmas will not have bad effects and good karmas will not have good effects. Every set of karmas have to give the corresponding effects, as karmas have no free will and cannot decide on their own whether to have an effect or not. It's the cosmic plan, not we, that decides when, how, where, and in what form the effects of individuals' karma manifest themselves. In the Bhagwat Gita, Lord Krishna has said: '*Karmanay vadhikaraste maa phaleshu kadachana . . .*' which means that we have the right to perform karma but have no right to decide the result of those karmas, nor any say in the manner, time, or form in which we reap them. That is decided by the cosmic forces depending on the various permutations and combinations of karmas performed. The cosmic forces might decide to give us result of our karma on a one-to-one basis or club several karmas and give one big result or split one karma into several results; it is their free will and choice and is hence unpredictable.

Any physical or mental action (a thought, imagination, or feeling) performed with the ego of doer-ship is called karma.

Karma creates deep-rooted impressions in the subconscious mind. These impressions remain in the subconscious mind till they are extinguished by a suitable result in the physical world or in the mental world.

Karmas are of three types—sanchit karma, prarabdh karma, and kriyamaan karma.

Sanchit karmas are the accumulated deposit of karmas that have not yet given their results and are waiting for an opportune time in the present or future births. Prarabdh karmas are a subset of Sanchit karmas which are responsible for the current birth. Based on these prarabdh karmas we encounter good and bad situations, happiness and sorrows, profit and loss in the present birth. This is what is also called fate or destiny. Prarabdh karmas are like the current account in a bank. These are drawn from the fixed deposit of Sanchit karmas. Kriyamaan karmas are the new karmas performed in the present birth.

Everything which has happened till now, everything which is happening right now, and everything which will happen in future is the result of, and will be the result of, our karmas. Nothing happens in life outside the Laws of Karma.

If we want to get rid of karmas and break the cycle of cause and effect, then we have to drop the ego of doer-ship. Doer-ship is the feeling that it is we who are doing an act. Even while performing all necessary activities, if we are free from doer-ship, then we will not be bound by karma and would not suffer the consequences of karma.

In a business there are many employees who perform their duties and responsibilities towards the owners of the business and, while going about their work, they are aware that all that they are doing is not for themselves but for the owner. Likewise, we also, while living in the world and while performing our duties and responsibilities should feel that we are representing the owner of the world, God—the Supreme Divine Being, and all our actions are performed on His behalf and not for our individual selves. We should attribute all our actions to Him and accept all life situations as a gift from Him as compensation for our efforts.

Just as the result of the effort of the employees is enjoyed or suffered solely by the business owner and not the employee, so will be the case with us. As the representative of the Supreme Divine Being, when we attribute all our actions to Him, then He becomes the enjoyer or sufferer of our actions and we remain free from the bondage of karma, as well as, free from the result of karma.

Say, we do a favour for a friend. Suppose the friend does not return the favour, we feel angry and disappointed. However, if we dedicate that very same favour to God, instead of the friend, we are freed from the burden of our expectation. If someone does us some harm, we feel sorrowful, angry, and vengeful towards that person. But instead, if we dedicate our suffering to God, we will be freed from these negative emotions. Thus, over a course of time, if we learn to dedicate our every action, thought and even the very breath we take to God, only then will we finally be free of the cycle of karma.

The attribution of our action should not just be intellectual; it should be done with a feeling of complete surrender and deep connection to the Supreme Divine Being. One has to always remain emotionally connected to the Supreme Divine Being with the feeling of love and devotion. In this state we will never ever perform any wrong action or sinful karmas because we will never dare to make our life owner, the Supreme Divine Being, suffer for our karmas. Remaining always connected with the Supreme Divine Being, we would only emanate love, compassion, care, and concern for all the beings equally, irrespective of their being related or unrelated to us.

One of the best examples to understand the state of non-doer-ship and remaining free from the bondage of karma even while performing karma can be found in the Mahabharata.

On the eve of the Great War, Arjuna was struck by doubts and indecision and wanted to withdraw from the war. He told Krishna, "I cannot kill my brothers, uncles, grandfather, guru, acharya, and relatives. Instead I would prefer to take sanyasa and live my life in seclusion in the forest."

Lord Krishna replied, "Even if you live in the forest and lead the life of a sanyasi, you will still be performing some actions and those actions will become your karma whose results you will have to enjoy or suffer. But now, in this war, while I am with you, if you fight the war considering yourself my representative and attribute all your actions to me, then neither will you be bound by karma, nor will you enjoy or suffer the result of those karmas."

A soldier fighting for his king or an army fighting for its country is not held responsible for their actions on the battlefield because they fight not for personal gain, but on behalf of the country. Similarly, *when we perform actions on behalf of the Supreme Divine Being we are not bound by any karma or its results.* Our actions will just remain actions without getting converted to karmas. Karma requires a doer-ship and we are freed of doer-ship by attributing our actions to the Supreme Divine Being. These actions would be termed as kriya and not karma.

Kriya is an action which is not bound by any result and karma is an action which is bound by a result.

Bathing, eating, walking, talking, washing, sleeping, and all such routine acts, are called kriyas as they do not give any corresponding result. We also don't expect any result out of these actions hence remain free from the Laws of Karma.

But in some religions, even these actions are considered as karmas as they attach virtues and sins to these actions too. When they are considered as karmas they are bound to give corresponding good or bad result too.

It is up to us to treat any action as kriya or karma. Kriya will not have any effect but karma will give corresponding result.

Kriya liberates and Karma binds.

Let all our actions be attributed to the Supreme Divine Being, while remaining surrendered to him and living our daily lives in the world as his representatives. When we perform actions with this feeling, we will never get entangled in the web of karmas. If you want to enjoy the bliss of liberation and lead a liberated life, convert your karma into kriya.

NECTAR OF GYANA:

- Know that nothing happens in this world accidentally and everything is pre-planned and perfectly planned.
- We enjoy and suffer in life based on our own karmas and no one other than we are responsible for our good fate or bad luck, favourable and unfavourable situations.
- No one can predict our future as every moment our fate is changing based on the actions and reactions we are performing.
- Be careful in performing karma as every karma will get its corresponding result in this birth or future births.
- Always think, imagine, and feel positive, as even thinking, imagining, and feeling will form karma.
- Seek forgiveness for causing any hurt to anyone as their negative vibrations can ruin our lives.
- Gradually make it a habit of offering karmas to God and accept the result of karma (favourable and

unfavourable) with love and devotion as a gracious gift from God and thereby enjoy the freedom and bliss of liberation.

The Joy of Fearlessness

The biggest enemy of human beings is 'fear' and all problems in life arise because of it. Fear takes away our peace, happiness, harmony, success, excitement, energy, and sleep. It clouds our potential to do bigger things in life and find the real purpose of life. In our everyday lives, we face many fears—fear of losing health, fear of losing wealth, fear of losing relationships, fear of losing our job, fear of losing peace, fear of losing physical pleasures, and fear of death.

FEAR is False Evidence Appearing Real. We see the ill health of others and worry about falling sick ourselves, although we are perfectly healthy. We see the misfortune of others and imagine that the same fate will befall us, though we are under no such threat. Thus, we project the experiences of others upon ourselves and these false experiences seem very real to us.

But let us look more closely at the very foundation of these fears. Fear arises when we consider something to be ours, i.e., when there is a feeling of ownership. When we know that we possess something only for a temporary period and for a specific purpose then we don't fear its loss as much as that of something we think of as permanent. In fact, when we know that something is available to us only for a temporary period then we enjoy it far more than if it was permanently available, as there would be no fear of losing it.

A cashier in a bank doesn't fear losing the cash he handles in large amounts every day. At the end of the day he puts back the remaining cash in the vault of the bank and goes home and sleeps peacefully. He has no fear of losing the money he left in the bank's vault.

Why not?

Because he knows that the money doesn't belong to him personally. He is only its custodian while he is in the service of the bank. He also knows that someone else, the security guards, are responsible for its safety. But if under ignorance he were to think of the money as his personal asset then he would definitely have sleepless nights and would live under the constant fear of losing it.

The biggest reason for fear is the feeling of ownership. Even though rational reasoning tells us that neither our physical body, nor our possessions, nor our relations will remain forever ours, we still labour under the ignorance that these things are permanent in nature and owned by us, and therefore we fear losing them.

There was once a king who lived in one of the most beautiful palaces of his times. One day he invited his spiritual master to the palace for dinner, but the real purpose was to show off his opulently gold-plated, diamond-studded, architecturally wonderful palace. After the master had his dinner the king took him around his palace. The master did not utter a single word of praise during the entire tour, but merely smiled, looking amused.

The king was upset by the master's lack of awe in the face of so much splendour. After some time, still fishing for compliments, the king asked the master how he found his palace.

The master asked, "Your palace, where is your palace?"

Surprised, the king retorted, "Everything I just showed you, everything you saw, is my palace, master!"

The master said, "My dear ignorant king! What you have just now shown me is only a dharamshala, a choultry, a temporary resting place, more like an inn or caravanserai for travellers and nothing more."

Taken aback, the king got a little upset and said, "How can you call my opulent palace a dharamshala, a choultry, a caravanserai!?"

The master then decided to ask him a few questions before explaining. "Who resided in this place before you became the king?"

The king said, "My father."

The master continued. "And who resided here before your father?"

The king replied, "My grandfather."

"And before your grandfather?" asked the master.

The king said, "My great-grandfather."

"And who will reside in this place after you?"

The king proudly announced, "My son!"

"And after your son who will occupy this place?" the master asked, and the king replied with assurance, "My grandson."

The master smiled. "So, my dear king! All your predecessors stayed here for some time and left and your future generations too will stay here for some time and leave, then how can this be called your palace? Any place where different people come, stay for some time, and leave is called dharamshala, a choultry. Hence how can you claim this place to be your palace?"

The king understood what his master was trying to convey. He realized his ignorance in considering the palace as his own.

In ignorance we think of many things as ours but actually they are available to us only for temporary usage, till we are alive in this world. Once we depart from this world we will have no connection with any of them. We will return in a different body, in another family, and in the midst of a completely new set of people and places. Once again in that new birth our ignorance will lay claim over our thoughts and we will start claiming many things as ours. In our previous birth also we must have claimed a physical body as ours, a family as ours, and a lot of wealth, property, and business assets as ours. But where has all that gone? Why don't we continue to claim those things as ours in the present birth? And through what means will we claim our present possessions in our future births?

The biggest attachment and feeling of ownership is with our physical body. Our entire life we equate our body with our true existence. We attach our 'I' existence to our physical body and consider everything associated through the physical body as 'My'—my parents, my spouse, my child, my house, my business, my country, my religion, my friend, my job, my clothes, my backyard, my dog . . . and so on.

Everything we associate with 'I' and 'My' vanishes in a moment with our last breath. The moment our soul exits with the death of the physical body all that which we considered 'I' and 'My' becomes a mere dream for it. Nothing remains with it, neither the physical body nor the physical matter and relations.

Such is the bitter reality of life.

Once there lived a king who had a young, smart, and intelligent son. He loved him the most. One day his beloved son died all of a sudden. The king's grief knew no bounds. Unable to control his grief, he even tried to kill himself but was saved by his queens and ministers. The king stopped going to his courtroom and stopped attending to his duties.

Everyone tried to persuade him to start taking care of himself and the kingdom but he couldn't be persuaded. His only wish was to see his son again.

At last, hearing about the pathetic condition of the king, the master arrived and tried to bring the king out of his grief by saying, "Everyone who comes to this world has to depart one day or the other." But king wouldn't heed to the master's wisdom too and kept crying that he wanted to see his son at least once.

Finally, the master agreed to call the son's soul and allow the king to talk to him.

With his mystic powers, the master invited the soul of the king's son to interact for some time with the king. Even as the king waited eagerly to hear his son, a stern angry voice was heard: "Who disturbed me and called me here?"

Realizing that it was his son's voice, the king, overcome by emotion, asked, "How are you, my son?"

"Son, whose son?" asked the voice in irritation.

"You are my son and I am your father, my son," said the king.

"What rubbish are you talking?" said the voice. "I was the son of so many fathers and I was the father of so many sons. You were son to me in so many births and I was your father and mother in many other births. You and I, we have both had hundreds of such relationships in our previous births. How can we claim to be father or son when we never had any permanent relationship with each other?

"Once we depart from the world we also get dropped and detached of all our relationships and possessions. I am on my own journey, oh king, and you may continue with yours. Our relationship was only till I was alive and not anymore. We were destined to be related to each other only for a short time."

Listening to this wisdom from his son's soul, the veil of king's ignorance was lifted and he came out of his grief.

'I' and 'my' is the cause and the seed of all the grief, miseries, and fears of life.

The fear of death coupled with fear of losing parents, spouse, children, house, wealth, status, name, fame and everything else to which we are connected to is so profound that we live life under constant stress. The objects, virtues, and relations that we call 'my' or use to define 'I', are the ones that lead us to fear as they are attached to the physical body. When the body dies, all of these objects, virtues, habits, thoughts, desires, and relations too die with it, leaving behind its impressions on the mind. The soul is just a carrier of the mind to the next birth.

The entire Bhagwat Gita and all the seven hundred shlokas by Lord Krishna are dedicated to dispelling this ignorance of 'I' and 'my' so as to liberate the soul from the various karmas, attractions, aversions, and fears it has acquired during the process of its various lives.

In one of the episodes of the Indian mythological epic Mahabharata, a Yakshaa demigod asks Yudhistara, the eldest of the Pandavas, what he thinks is the most surprising thing in human beings.

And Yudhistara replies, "The most surprising thing in humans is that every moment hundreds of people die all over the world and those who survive think that only those have died, who were destined to die. Next moment among the same survivors hundreds more die and those who survive think that only those people have died who were destined to die. No one ever thinks that they could also be destined to die among the next lot of deaths. Everyone thinks that they are going to live long and only others are going to die."

If a reliable source were to predict our death within the next day or week or month, then the way we live life would undergo a drastic change. Our perceptions, behaviour, and attitude towards people and the world would undergo a complete changeover. We would become peaceful, more resilient and loving and, in all probability, turn towards God too. All worldly matters and aspirations would take a back seat. We would drop all our vices and bad habits. We would give away our possessions to others. We would apologise for our wrongdoings, misbehaviour, and for the hurt we have caused to others, and try to make amends. We would want to delete from our mind all the negative and positive impressions so that we can depart from this world with an unburdened mind.

A disciple used to visit his master regularly and seek his blessings and advice to get rid of his bad habits, anger, and lust, and to meditate upon God. Yet, despite repeated advice and instruction, he seemed unable to apply his master's teachings in his life.

One day when the disciple visited the master and repeated the same request, the master in a sad voice told him that he was going to die in a week's time

Taken aback at such an unexpected prediction from the master, the disciple went back home in despair. He remained at home for all the remaining seven days and left everything to his sons and wife to handle. He stopped fighting and annoying people and kept meditating upon God all the time. He felt completely at peace with his inner self.

On the seventh day, the last day of his life, he went to the master to seek his blessings for one last time. He was calm, serene, and appeared to have realized his own self, *the God within.*

Seeing his disciple in this state, the master got up from his seat and hugged him. When the master enquired about his bad habits, vices, anger, and mediation practice, the disciple fell at the feet of the master and thanked him for making him realize his true identity and helping him in his reunion with God.

When it was time for the disciple to take leave of his master he touched his feet to seek his blessings.

The master smiled and said, "May you live long, my son."

The disciple looked at the master in surprise. He reminded his master that it was the last day of his life as predicted by him.

"Consider every day as the last day of your life, my dear son, and live life joyfully, as some day is truly going to be the last day of our life."

This is what we need to think every day. Live every day as if it were the last day of our lives and see how beautiful life is without any attractions and aversions, without any hatred and enmity, without jealousy and comparison, without any negative feeling for anyone. There will only be love, forgiveness, and joy all around.

Death is the most unpredictable subject of our existence and it strikes in the most unexpected ways. No one is sure of one's life pattern, nor do we have any choice in the date, day, time, place and the manner in which we will die and depart.

We don't know when death will come for us. All of us, in our own little circle of life, have seen people dying when they were least expected to. Death is cruel and merciless, as it has no consideration for young or old, rich or poor, male or female, child or parent. It can strike anyone, anytime, anywhere, and in any manner.

We have seen children dying before their parents, young ones dying in front of elders, healthy people dying before people who were sick and expected to die first. And we have seen people dying while returning home from office to be with the family, while playing sports, while entertaining people, while praying in places of worship, while strolling on the streets, and when it was most unforeseeable.

Nobody wants to think of one's death in spite of knowing that death doesn't knock at our doors before attacking and generally doesn't often give much advance intimation. But the reason we truly fear death is because no one knows what happens after death. It is more a fear of the unknown than a fear of death itself.

If we can experience death while being alive all our fears and dismay would vanish. We would live life more peacefully and enjoyably. And this is possible if we can experience *the true state of our being, the soul as separate from the physical body.*

It is said face your fears and watch them turn their back on you. Then why not face the fear of death while being alive, by letting the soul detach from the physical body? Whether or not we acknowledge it, we are getting close to our physical death with every second that passes, so why not be aware of our real state of being before we die?

The soul is the driving force behind the physical body. The physical body takes birth, grows, decays, and eventually dies, but the soul remains the same, unchanging and immortal. The soul neither takes birth nor grows nor decays nor becomes old nor dies.

After the death of the physical body, the soul leaves the body and remains in space. Depending on the impressions of karma on its mind, it waits in the cosmos to acquire a relevant body where it can settle the accounts of its karmas.

This fact, even if known to people through the reading of scriptures or by listening to discourses, remains just intellectual information and nothing more than that. It can be fully believed only when we experience the existence of the soul as separate from the physical body.

This experience is possible through repeatedly listening to the discourses of enlightened beings, yogic sadhana, contemplation, nididhyasana, meditation, samadhi, or through the grace of a guru. Swami Vivekananda went into samadhi and experienced this soul state, separate from the physical body, just by the touch of the feet of his guru Ramakrishna Paramahansa.

In yogic sadhana, one can experience the separation of the soul from the physical body and achieve a state wherein the soul leaves and returns to the body at will.

This practice helps us achieve a state of detachment from the physical body as we experience the temporary nature of the physical body, the specific purpose for which the body is acquired and the fact of remaining alive as soul even after the death of the body. This makes the soul fearless of death and once it becomes fearless it starts enjoying its life to the fullest extent.

Once we overcome the fear of death then we would naturally overcome our attachment to material objects such as wealth, property, status, name, fame, business and relations and live a blissful life while enjoying everything in the physical plane.

Fear is fearful of fearlessness. Fear gets dispelled through gyana. Gyana is all about the existence of a soul separate from the body. Gyana is about the eternity of the soul and the perishability of the physical body and physical matter. Be fearless and enjoy life.

Nectar of gyana:

- Fear is born out of ignorance and caused by attributing permanence to things that are only temporary.

- Know that you are not the owner of anything in this world, not even your physical body. You are just a temporary custodian of all your possessions.

- You have not brought anything in this world when you were born and you will not take anything with you when you depart from this world. Everything is acquired here and will be left behind in this world.

- Know that you are the soul, an entity separate from the physical body, and that the soul will remain alive even after the death of the body. Do not fear death as that is certain to come one day.
- Always be ready for a peaceful death by being peaceful all the time as what you practice while being alive is what will reflect on your soul at the time of death.

Emotion of Devotion

*T*o *become prayerless during prayer is the highest order of prayer.*

When Ramakrishna Paramahansa used to worship Maa Kali, he would gradually forget that he was sitting before Maa Kali and worshipping her. Sometimes, he would stop worshipping midway and at other times he would worship himself, showering flower petals on his own head and performing aarti for himself. Sometimes he would forget the rituals altogether and go into a trance.

Devotion should be of such intensity that one forgets that he and his God are two separate entities. We should become one with God. This is real bhakti, the emotion of devotion.

Japa, repetition of mantras, hymns, prayers, homa, yagya, puja of an idol or yantra, and worship are to be used only as tools to lead the mind from many thoughts towards one thought and eventually to become one with the worshipped.

Initially one may worship God in any aspect—form or formless—through external actions such as prayers, gestures, oblations, aarti (rotating a lighted lamp), bhakti, bhajans, prostrations, and other forms of rituals, but later, one must shift the focus of worship from the *external to the internal* in the form of contemplation, meditation, and surrender.

At the time of Buddha, there lived an old beggar woman. She used to watch kings, princes, and the common people making offerings to Buddha and his disciples, and there was nothing she would have liked more than to be able to do the same. So, she went out begging, but at the end of a whole day all she had was one small coin. She took it to the oil merchant to buy some oil. When he heard that she wanted it to make an offering to Buddha, he took pity on her and gave her the oil she wanted.

She took the oil to the monastery, where she lit a lamp. She placed it before Buddha and made a wish: "I have nothing to offer but this tiny lamp. But through this offering, in the future may I be blessed with the lamp of wisdom. May I free all beings from their darkness. May I purify all their obstructions and lead them to enlightenment."

That night the oil in all the other lamps finished. But the beggar woman's lamp still burned at dawn, when Buddha's disciple Maudgalyayana came to collect the lamps. When he saw that it was still alight, full of oil and with a new wick, he thought, "There's no reason why this lamp should still be burning in the day time," and he tried to blow it out. But it kept on burning. He tried to snuff it out with his fingers, but it stayed alight. He tried to smother it with his robe, but it still remained enkindled.

Buddha had been watching all along, and said, "Maudgalyayana, do you want to put out that lamp? You cannot. You cannot even move it, let alone put it out. If you were to pour water from all oceans over this lamp, it still wouldn't go out. The water in all the rivers and the lakes of the world could not extinguish it."

"Why not?" asked Maudgalyayana.

"Because this lamp was offered with devotion, surrender, and purity of heart and that has made it tremendously powerful."

When Buddha said this, the beggar woman approached Him, and He made a prophecy that in the future she would become a perfect Buddha, called 'Light of the Lamp'.

Devotion means to surrender. Surrender to the will of God. Devotion is one of the best methods to divert one's attention from worldly activities and increase focus towards God. In real devotion, one forgets the strict conditions of rituals and defined patterns of worshipping. One goes beyond the realm of right or wrong, good or bad, and gets so emotionally connected to God that for the worshipper there is only God and God's bhakti in the mind.

In one of the episodes of the famous epic Ramayana, Shabari, who was a bhakt, a staunch devotee of Rama, offered berries to Rama after tasting each one of them, giving only the sweet ones to Rama and casting the sour ones away. Lakshmana protested that the berries that had already been partially eaten by Shabari were unworthy offerings to the lord. To this Rama said, "Of the many types of food I have eaten in my lifetime, nothing can equal the taste of these berries."

God responds to devotion, not rituals. God can never be realized through rituals as they become mechanical over a period of time. Rituals are created to emanate devotion. They are merely the ladder to devotion, but people ignorantly consider them to be the ultimate form of worship of God.

When Lord Krishna went to meet Duryodhana to make peace before the Mahabharata war, Duryodhana invited Lord Krishna to have dinner with him. Lord Krishna declined, saying, "One accepts an invitation for dinner only under two circumstances–either one is hungry, or the host is a devotee. In this case, however, neither am I hungry nor are you my devotee."

From there Lord Krishna went to the house of Vidur. Both Vidur and his wife were his ardent devotees. When Lord Krishna sat down to dinner, Vidur's wife offered him bananas. Lord Krishna asked her to feed Him with her own hands. Tears of joy flowed from her eyes as she peeled the bananas and, in her rapture, she offered the peels to Krishna instead of the bananas. Lord Krishna ate the peels, joyfully and without complaint.

When God is worshipped with such devotion, God goes beyond all the prescribed norms to honour that devotion and to protect the devotee too.

However, the highest order of worship is the worship the *eternal formless pure consciousness* and not the worship of a limited form. Since the entire creation, including all living beings and forms, have manifested out of pure consciousness, worshipping the pure consciousness is as good as worshipping the entire manifestation.

Worshipping a deity in its limited aspect may yield results in the limited form of fulfilment of worldly desires but worshipping God in His pure consciousness formless state and all-pervading aspect results in becoming one with Him.

In this form of worship every action gets dedicated and attributed to the consciousness, to the extent that even while eating food it is deemed to be eaten by the consciousness itself, lying down in any manner is deemed as prostration to the consciousness, loving any creature is deemed as loving the consciousness, walking is considered as encompassing the consciousness, seeing anything is considered as seeing the consciousness and so on. There cannot be a greater worship than this.

When consciousness is the deity of worship then everybody in the universe is worshipped because everybody is born to the consciousness, and everything has manifested from the consciousness, and consciousness itself has become everything and everybody, hence there is no need to worship any particular deity limited to any one form. In this worship one's vision changes to such an extent that one sees in everyone and in everything the same consciousness acting differently and in different ways.

Once a saint walking on the street was accidentally struck by a vehicle and he fell down. He was taken to the hospital by a bystander. He smilingly said to the doctor treating him, "You first hit me and make me fall, then bring me to the hospital and then you treat me as well. What kind of maya is this?"

The doctor in his amusement says, "No, babaji. It was not I who hit you nor was I the one to bring you to the hospital. They were different people. I am only treating you."

To this, the saint smiled and said, "I know your ploy. You only play different characters at different times in different places."

This was the state of the saint, seeing everyone as consciousness and everything as the play of consciousness.

Once when the great saint Namdev was making roti, a dog came from somewhere, picked one and ran away. Namdev ran behind it with a bowl of ghee, saying, "God, please apply some ghee on the roti or else you will have to eat it dry." This kind of vision and perception of seeing the same God, the same consciousness, in everyone is rare and is of the highest order.

Some people sacrifice animals and such in the worship of their favourite deity, thinking this would please the deity who will then bestow upon them its blessings. How can God be happy with such offerings made through violent acts? God is a divine entity full of compassion, equal care, and unconditional love for all. *The biggest sacrifice one can offer is of one's ego and its synonyms.* Once this ego is forgone all that remains is the pure soul worthy of becoming one with his creator.

Devotion is a state of internal emotion. It is the flow of emotion, love, and joy towards the supreme god. Devotion is not something which is projected outside to be seen by others nor is it based on physical movements such as circumambulation of a temple or deity, rotating a lighted lamp in aarti, clapping, dancing, or calling out to God loudly. On the contrary, it is personal and inward-looking, a state of intense mental delight.

Let devotion flow naturally through the emotions. Do not bind it with unnatural acts, rituals, and any sort of restrictive practices. Enjoy divinity at all times and in every place. Know that divine grace has been showered on you. Believe in it and bask in its glory.

God is the eternal, all-pervading consciousness, and everybody is driven by this consciousness. The process of creation first emanated sparks of consciousness called atman, the self. This then emanated life force, the prana. The life force, prana, then emanated five basic elements that we know as ether, air, fire, water, and earth. These five elements combined together in different proportions and created the gross world such as earth, moon, sun, planets, mountains, trees, water, environment, and various creatures. The whole universe and all creatures are nothing but modified forms of the source of all creation, the pure consciousness.

Thus, in everything in the universe there exists pure consciousness, and in pure consciousness exists the entire universe.

The Vedas say *'Yatha brahmande, tatha pindande'* meaning everything which exists in the cosmos exists in our physical bodies and anything which exists in the physical body exists in the cosmos too. Everything from ether, air, fire, water, earth to sun, moon, stars, heaven, hell, and gods all are present in the physical body.

As all the gods too exist in the physical body, *the physical body is called a moving temple* in the Vedas. These scriptures advise us not to look outside ourselves for our desires and for God. Just turn inwards and whatever you want is already within you.

These Vedas have further declared that whatever does not exist in the physical body, the pindanda, does not exist in the cosmos either, the brahmanda. So, if we cannot find someone within the body to worship, then we cannot find it outside either.

When God is accepted as consciousness and everything in creation as consciousness, then whatever one worships, one must have the bhava of worshipping the consciousness and not worshipping the object. The Vedas have said that with whatever bhava one worships, one would achieve and become that. However, if we worship the formless consciousness, then we will merge into the consciousness and get liberated from the cycle of birth, death, and rebirth.

Nectar of gyana:

- Recognize the power of devotion. Do not get bound by rituals, but worship God with devotion.
- The whole of creation is a modified form of consciousness, so see the consciousness in everything and every being.
- We are all moving temples dedicated to the Supreme Divine Being residing in our hearts. Behave with everyone as if behaving with the Supreme Divine Being.
- If you worship the form, you will come back to the form. If you worship the formless, you will merge with the formless and get liberated.

Who is He?

I don't believe in rituals and idol worship. If God is restricted to temples and other places of worship, then I don't want to go to him, and, on the other hand, if God is present everywhere, then I don't need to go anywhere to find Him.

I always strongly believed that God meant some power or energy not restricted to a form, which is the cause of the creation of this universe. This energy and power is infinite, formless, omnipresent and omnipotent, and is available to us at all times and at all places without any restrictions whatsoever, for us to fall back on for support, to look for life solutions, to seek a way out when there seems to be no end to suffering, and to worship for our personal and spiritual evolution.

Most people think of God as a superhuman entity with tremendous supernatural powers, who has descended on earth at various times in the past through avatars to destroy evil forces, to establish dharma, and to protect his bhakt. The faith of these people is mostly attached to the supernatural acts performed by these gods and they are worshipped for their blessings and protection.

They also fear that if they do not worship God regularly, and in the prescribed format, then God will get angry and will withdraw His support and protection. So to keep the gods happy and to be in their good books, these believers worship their favourite gods daily, either in temples, puja rooms at home, sacred places, or at places where God has supposedly visited in the past.

Though I do not subscribe to these beliefs, neither have I ever belittled the faith of others in any particular form of God or deity, as I understood that it's all a matter of one's belief system. Everyone has a right over their belief system and is free to worship anybody of their choice. But personally, I could never limit God to any particular roopa, or finite form. I enjoy feeling the presence of God everywhere—as space, as air, invisible and available to me, just a thought away.

He was never far away from me, never required any particular method of worship from me, was always available to guide and show me the right path whenever I was stuck, always moving with me and enjoying being around me. He was like an invisible genie, who would say, "Your intention is my command, my son."

Thanks to this *bhava* and idea, I never had any interest

in visiting temples, other than for enjoying the serenity and positive vibrations of the place and also for the sumptuous prasad offered in most places.

Because normal human minds are limited in nature, limited in thinking, and limited in their comprehension; they have no time, energy, and inquisitiveness to see God beyond what they comprehend in a particular form. Everyone is busy in their own world, struggling to make ends meet, or engrossed in worldly affairs, so much so that investing their energies in knowing who God really is seems futile to them.

Most people, in spite of not being sure if the God they worship really exists or not, blindly and faithfully worship Him just because many others do so.

Irrespective of whether God exists or not, and irrespective of what form He is worshipped in, what works is faith. Faith has power. Faith can move mountains. Faith can perform miracles. And it is this faith that comes to the rescue of people who worship God without knowing or seeing or feeling His existence in their lifetime.

But as our minds are fickle and our faith depends mostly on the success of materialistic desires, chances are high that our faith might shift from one God to another or be lost completely in all forms of God if our desires are not fulfilled. When one loses faith, the power attached to faith also gets lost or diminished.

In the old Hindu tradition, there was a practice of *sati* followed in some parts of India. It mandated that upon the death of the husband, the wife too would offer herself up, to be burnt alive on the funeral pyre of the husband.

In one such incidence in a remote village, as the widow sat on the burning pyre of her husband, a heavy storm with thunder and lightning struck the place. The gathered people all ran for cover. Seeing everyone running away, the widow too jumped down from the burning pyre and ran into the nearby forest. The storm was such that it washed away the pyre and the half-burnt corpse into the nearby river.

Next morning, when the villagers returned to the pyre, they found nothing there except some traces of burnt wood. They considered the whole episode a miracle and built a temple dedicated to the widow who had committed Sati, installed her idol and named the temple 'Maa Sati Mandir'.

People started offering prayers, coconuts, flowers, fruits, and money at the temple. Gradually people began to have their wishes and desires fulfilled. As word spread about the miraculous powers the temple had, more people started flocking there. Soon it became famous all over the country. The temple too became rich in wealth from all the offerings made by the visitors.

One day, while travelling to another village, one of the villagers saw a poor woman sweeping the surroundings of her hut. As he was thirsty he approached the woman for some water. That's when he realized that this was the same woman who was being worshipped in the temple as the deity.

Upon enquiry the woman revealed the whole story as to how she had jumped off her husband's pyre and run away when she saw everyone running away in the storm and how she had managed to reach this hamlet and, with the help of some people, had settled here by doing odd jobs in some houses. She was just managing to make both ends meet.

She was completely unaware of what was happening in her village and the temple that had been built in her name and the large crowds flocking there. She had become a famous deity, renowned for fulfilling the wishes of the faithful. While many people became rich after offering their prayers in that temple, she, the main deity of the temple, was herself surviving with great difficulty.

The traveller returned to his village and shared this information with other villagers. As people became aware that the sati they had been worshipping was in fact alive, they lost faith and stopped going to the temple. As people lost faith in the sati temple, the power of the deity of the temple too got lost and nobody's wishes were fulfilled thereafter. Soon, the famous temple became a neglected ruin.

This is how our faith works. The real power is not in the idol or place of worship but in our faith itself. Why then should we restrict our faith to a particular place, form, or pattern of worship or prayer? Why not remove such pre-conditions and keep faith switched ON at all times, in all places, and in all kinds of situations?

Do we really love God in the true sense? If we did, wouldn't the loved one be in our hearts at all times? Why, then, do we keep Him less in our heart and more confined to puja rooms, temples, and other places of worship?

Once some saints were passing through a forest and they saw someone sitting dejectedly on a hillock. Unable to clearly see who it was, they called out, "Who are you? What is the matter?"

The reply came, "I am God, and I have been thrown out of my house."

"How can anyone throw you out of your house? We do not understand what you are saying," said the saints.

"My house is in the heart of all the beings, but humans have thrown me out of their hearts and kept me locked up in temples and puja rooms," said God, "and so I am feeling lonely and sad."

This is precisely what we humans have done to God. Not only have we conveniently put Him out of our hearts, but we have put Him in places where we are unlikely to visit Him or visit Him less often.

Take the puja room, for instance. It is usually the smallest room in our houses, not ventilated at all, and sometimes with no place to even sit comfortably. All this leads to the conclusion that people worship God as a mere ritual performed out of fear and greed. They never feel the real presence of God in the places of worship or at home. Even the oblation, or naivedyam, that we offer God is made as per our tastes. If we eat spicy food we cook spicy food and offer it to God and if we eat bland food we offer the same to God, irrespective of what God wants to eat. If we worshipped Him with the right bhava and genuinely felt His presence, then wouldn't we behave accordingly and accord Him the highest status in the household, the choicest food, the best room, and the best of facilities?

We know that God doesn't really exist where we think He exists. We know that His address is different and the actual place of His residence is different.

The question which my mind would always ask is, "Has anyone seen God?"

God has been largely believed to be a superbeing with supernatural powers who lives up in the sky, though no one knows exactly where this 'up' is. He is believed to be always available to us to fulfil our personal aspirations. We try to please God by lighting candles, incense sticks or lamps, by offering coconuts and sweets. Of course, no one knows what God would do with so many coconuts, sweets, flowers, or leaves.

Another question that bothered me was with respect to fasting. I could never understand why God should be pleased to see us hungry, when we are His children. No parent would feel pleased to see his or her children starve.

And the best part is we believe God fulfils our desires and aspirations without even questioning us if they are for our need or greed, and without even bothering to know if we will use them for right or wrong purposes. He doesn't even bother to know if we will use whatever He gives us or misuse and abuse it.

I sometimes wonder how foolishly we fool ourselves thinking that we are fooling God. Rarely does anyone worship God out of love, it's all out of greed or fear. *Unfortunately, most of us are God-fearing people and not God-loving people.*

Those who really love God are not bound by rituals and do not restrict their worship to a particular place or format. Love is boundless and knows no limitations. Love doesn't demand anything from the loved one. Love doesn't expect anything in return. Therefore, those who love unconditionally never feel disappointed or betrayed even when adversity strikes them.

To understand God, we will have to apply some logic to our discussions. If God ever existed in any of the physical forms that we comprehend Him in, then who created God in the first place? Is God self created? If God is self created then God has to have another state of Himself, before His own physical creation, through which HE could create Himself. And that state through which God could create Himself has to be even more powerful than the created God. It has to be all-powerful, omnipresent, and omnipotent; how else would it create so many gods in different places, at different times, in different forms and with different powers for different purposes. It has to be something beyond physical limitation and beyond time, space, and matter.

Only a Formless, Omnipresent, Omnipotent Entity can be the real creator of all creation. One cannot be a Creator when He Himself is limited by a form.

Let us try to understand God a little differently. The word GOD is basically an acronym for three energies that are eternally present in the universe and are responsible for all the aspects of creation. They are:

G=Generation

O=Operation

D=Destruction

In the Hindu tradition, these three energies are identified in three forms as Brahma, Vishnu, and Mahesh. Brahma, the Generator (creator), Vishnu the Operator (Preserver), and Mahesh or Shiva, the Destroyer.

These three gods represent these three energies and the forms in which they are familiar to us are mere representations to help uninitiated minds understand the working of these three energies.

These energies are part of the super consciousness, the main source and cause of all creation. Super consciousness is Formless, Eternal, Omnipresent, and Omnipotent. It is what is known as brahmanda in the Vedas.

Let God not be restricted to a particular form. Even though there is nothing wrong in worshipping God in a limited form of our choice, yet perceiving God as Energy or as consciousness or as atman, and paramatma, which resides in our hearts, will make things much easier for us. We can carry God with us all the time without restricting Him to a particular place and time. In this way, we can go through life, secure in the knowledge that God is with us 24x7 till our last breath and even after that, with our immortal soul.

Nectar of gyana:

- Let us not restrict the infinite to the finite and limit God to a particular form, place, or mode of worship. Keep Him in your heart and feel Him walk, talk, eat, act, react, and be with you at all times.
- Know that He needs love, not rituals.
- Look to God for personal evolution and joyful living and not for worldly desire fulfilment.
- Let's use the power of Generation for generating joy, power of Operation for maintaining and spreading that joy, and the power of Destruction for destroying hatred, jealousy, enmity, and other negativity of the mind.

Infinite Potential
in the Finite

You have two options to live life. Either have control over emotions or allow emotions to control your life.

The mind is the most fascinating and complex thing to exist in this universe. The mind is the dynamic aspect of consciousness. It is a powerhouse in itself. It can think, ponder, contemplate, reflect, understand, accept or reject, form opinions, believe, disbelieve, guess, judge, conceive, surmise, suspect, imagine, reckon and visualize, create impressions, delete impressions, and carry forward impressions for immeasurable lengths of time.

The mind can make human beings enjoy their lives or make them suffer. It can cause pains and pleasures. It can create happiness and sorrow. It has the power to become what it thinks. It has the potential to create and destroy.

The mind is the point where pure static consciousness modifies into dynamic energy of consciousness. The mind operates at three levels of modifying consciousness—consciousness, sub consciousness, and unconsciousness. They are also termed as awakened state, dream state, and deep sleep state respectively.

It is in the nature of the mind to not remain peaceful, stable, still, or thoughtless for long. It does not require any effort to create stress, tension, conflict, anger, fear, negativity, sorrow, or impatience.

Negativity is like a gravitational force for the mind and if the mind is not kept positive and not trained to be positive it has a natural tendency to be pulled down by this gravitational force of negativity.

The mind is the main cause of bondage into the cycle of birth, death, and rebirth. The mind is also the main source for liberation. If properly guided and handled with care, it can help us enjoy the joys of life and remain in a blissful and liberated state.

The mind has the capability of reversing its negativity, but this requires a little effort. By exposing the mind to higher spiritual knowledge, especially of its original source, its nature, and its hidden potential, it can be trained to become positive, peaceful, joyful, loving, caring, decisive, and successful.

When the mind's performance is not up to the mark and it is not achieving its objectives, it only means it is operating in ignorance at a low potential. *Ignorance is nothing but the lack of sufficient knowledge or the non-acceptance of higher knowledge.*

When we operate in ignorance, our potential automatically gets reduced and we operate at lower levels than what we are capable of. Numerous studies have proved that an ordinary person operates at less than 5% of his potential and a successful person operates at around 10% of his potential. For most people, the balance 90% of potential remains unutilized and dies with the death of the body. However, spiritual sadhakas, yogis, siddha purusha, and enlightened souls know how to tap this hidden potential.

TECHNIQUES TO INVOKE HIGHER POTENTIAL FROM 5% TO 10%:

1. Positive Affirmations: Whenever possible, mentally chant positive affirmations such as 'I am happy', 'I am peaceful', 'I am successful', 'I am a good decision maker', 'My memory is great', 'I love everyone', 'Everyone loves me', 'I am divine', etc.

2. Be a Visionary: Visualize and emanate positive emotions about your goals. Visualization expands our narrow mind. It allows us to think beyond our present. An expanded mind is able to invoke higher potential.

3. Seek forgiveness: We must regularly seek forgiveness from all those whom we have knowingly or unknowingly hurt as their negative vibrations have the power to bring miseries, untoward incidents, and adversities in our life.

4. Meditation: Regular meditation helps the mind break its chain of thoughts and get into silence mode. A mind that is silent is a thousand times more powerful than a mind which is thoughtful. One-minute meditation, five to six times a day, also, is a great technique to make the mind habituated to get into peaceful mode at regular intervals.

The simplest meditation technique is to close your eyes and focus on the tip of your nostrils, watching your breath going in and going out.

Through these techniques higher potential powers of our mind get invoked, resulting in success in all the spheres of our life—be it professional, business, relationships, or spirituality. We become fearless, positive, decisive, and habituated to learning from adversities and moving forward in life.

Once some journalists asked a successful person what the secret of his success was, and the successful person replied, "Two words."

When asked what those two words were, he said, "Right decisions."

"But, sir, what is the secret of taking right decisions?"

"One word," replied the businessman.

"And what is that?"

"Experience," said the businessman.

"But, sir, how do you get experience?" asked one journalist.

"Two words," replied the businessman.

"And what are those two words, sir?"

"Wrong decisions!" said the businessman.

The real secret, unknown to many, of success is remaining aligned to the goal through the ups and downs and having constant belief in its achievement. This alone has the power to attract all that which one aims at in life.

When Einstein was removed from his school—as he was a weak student in science—his mother believed in him and also made him believe that he could do it. She took up the challenge of training him in science. We all know the result of that belief—he became one of the biggest scientists of his time.

All successful people in the world have unknowingly invoked this power of *belief* in them and that alone is the secret of their success. Without the power of belief however much effort we put in to achieve something, it will not bring the desired results. Every effort has to have this power of belief attached to it for a successful result.

Intense prayers and superstitious beliefs too have this 'power of belief' attached to them. The word *belief* attached to 'superstitious' itself is proof that it's the belief which works and not the superstition itself.

When we pray to God with intensity, we get connected to Him—the three energies of Generation, Operation, and Destruction—through our emotions. The vibrations, which we emanate with the intensity of our prayers, strengthen in the cosmos and eventually when a sufficient quantity of vibrations gets accumulated in the cosmos our prayers get answered.

There are many Indian girls who fast sixteen Mondays—Somvar Vrat—desiring to marry a perfect life partner. Monday is considered to be Lord Shiva's day and it is believed among Hindus, more specifically in southern India, that fasting on these days will get them a perfect husband, like Lord Shiva.

Another auspicious day assumed for fasting, particularly for unmarried girls, is the Swarna Gauri Vratam. Gauri is another name for Goddess Parvati and Vratam means fast. It is dedicated to Goddess Parvati, the consort of Lord Shiva.

The story behind this custom is as follows: Parvati wanted to marry Lord Shiva but Shiva did not reciprocate to her longing as he was mourning the death of his wife Sati. Parvati was determined to win Lord Shiva's love, so she practiced intense austerities in a forest, surviving on grass and fruits. Parvati continued this intense sadhana for sixteen years. Finally, Lord Shiva was moved by her intense devotion and love and married her.

Some people even vow to offer their hair to God, at a particular temple, upon fulfilment of their wishes. They continue to grow their hair till their desire gets fulfilled. While following such practices their attention is always on their excessively grown hair, which constantly reminds them of their intense desire to achieve some goal.

Secret: It's not for the fast, or the dedication of hair, that God answers our prayers. It is our constant remembrance of the desire, coupled with our strong belief that God will fulfil our desire that is the main cause of desire fulfilment.

It is actually the belief that works, not the medium through which the belief gets invoked. People ignorant of this science and secret believe the medium to be powerful rather than the power of their belief. Because of this ignorance, many astrologers, numerologists, palmists, face readers, tantriks, and pseudo sadhus trap the gullible for their own selfish interest and cash in on their superstitious beliefs.

There once lived a saint who was a staunch devotee of Lord Rama. One day one of his disciples wanted to go to the other side of the river for some urgent work but couldn't find a boat to cross the river. So, the saint wrote something on a piece of paper, folded it and gave it to the disciple saying that it is a very powerful mantra which can give him the power to walk on water.

Believing in the power of the saint and his mantra, the disciple went to the river and started walking on it. Halfway across he began to wonder what the powerful mantra was that could make him walk on the river. So, he opened the folded paper. He was bewildered to see only the name 'Rama' written on the paper and not any mantra. Disbelieving that only the name 'Rama' had the power to allow him to walk across the river, he drowned immediately.

The saint only invoked the power of belief in the disciple and that made it possible for him to do the impossible task of walking on water. As long as the disciple believed that he could walk on water with the mantra he had in his pocket, he was able to walk. Only when he doubted the efficacy of the name 'Rama', he stopped believing that he could walk any further across the river. His disbelief suppressed his power of belief and drowned him.

So, we should realize the potential power of our belief and use it unconditionally without any medium for goal achievements and the cosmic forces will definitely respond.

As the mind is the spark of pure consciousness, it has all the properties, qualities, and creative powers of God. At the macro level it is the *cosmic mind* which creates, operates, and destroys the universal world and at the micro level it is our individual mind which creates, operates, and destroys our personal world.

The mind is the God to its thoughts, first as the creator, then as the sustainer, and eventually as the destroyer of its own thoughts. It may emanate a thought to go for a movie and then it contemplates on which movie to go for, what time to go, whether tickets will be available for the movie or not, will there be any traffic problems, what to eat, where to eat, or whether to come back home and have dinner. Through these thoughts it sustains its original thought of going for a movie. The thought of going for a movie is destroyed by either completing that task or by emanating another thought of dropping the idea of going for the movie or a thought of going to meet a friend or to a party instead. Once again it sustains the new thought and destroys it after some time through the same process. It acts with all the three Godly energies—Generation, Operation, and Destruction for its own life situations.

Being a spark of pure consciousness, the mind carries

all the properties and powers of its source. Just as a drop of the ocean represents the entire ocean and carries all the properties of the ocean, similarly the mind, which is a drop of consciousness represents the omnipresent pure consciousness and carries all its properties and potential.

A drop of blood has all the information of the body in which it lives, such as the count of red blood cells, white blood cells, functioning of various organs of the body, oxygen levels, protein levels, infections in the body, and its DNA.

Similarly, an individual's mind is capable of indicating, conveying, and revealing everything that exists in the universe, what existed in the universe, what is going to happen, secrets of the working of the universe, how it came into existence, how it operates and eventually how it will merge back into its source.

This mind is capable of revealing the axis of the earth, rotation of moon around the earth, and their combined rotations around the sun. It can also reveal the distances of various planets, etc. In fact, all this information is precisely given in the Indian Vedas and has been acknowledged by modern scientists too. All these revelations took place during deep meditative states of Indian rishis and munis when their minds became one with the investigated object or one with the cosmic mind.

When the mind's thought process is cut off and it is made completely silent through long and intense meditation it becomes one with its source—the pure consciousness. When the mind becomes one with its source, it itself becomes the expanded pure consciousness and when it regains its individuality as an individual mind it comes back with all the information from its source. This is how revelations take place about the universe and its various aspects.

Once the mind starts becoming one with its source it enjoys its bliss and naturally becomes as powerful as the source itself. In fact, the bliss and the cosmic power were predominant when the mind first got separated from the all-pervasive pure consciousness, but over time its own flickering and restless nature suppressed the power.

Only when the flickering and restless nature of the mind is changed to peace and calm, and the mind expands to become one with its source, it regains its original state of being all-knowing, all-seeing, all-perceiving, and all-powerful.

This is when our potential grows beyond the usual 10% wherein supernatural power gets invoked. These powers may appear supernatural to common people but for a yogi it is simply a natural state.

Through intense spiritual sadhana, yogis and enlightened beings naturally acquire this state of the supernatural such as telepathy, vak siddhi (whatever is spoken comes true), vichar siddhi (whatever is thought of that comes true), prescience (ability to see future events before they actually occur), third-eye vision, awakening of kundalini shakti, bringing the soul out of body at will, samadhi—(being in meditation for long periods sometimes running into years at a stretch), becoming invisible and visible at will, being in two or more physical bodies simultaneously, creating an object from nothing, making oneself invisible at one place and visible at another place at the same time, astral travel, and many such supernatural acts.

Techniques to invoke potential powers beyond 10%:

This is tough as it requires a lot of patience, perseverance, and intense spiritual practice. One has to control one's senses by cutting off the subjects from their senses, withdrawal from worldly attractions, practice of celibacy, intense pranayama and meditation for long hours, awakening of kundalini shakti, eating only satvik food, asana siddhi, practicing yogic kriyas to cleanse the body at regular intervals, speaking a bare minimum and retreating into solitude at regular intervals especially in mountains, caves, or forests.

(It is advised and cautioned that all the above practices need to be practiced under the expert guidance of spiritual masters, as these practices are highly technical and have long-term repercussions if not followed properly. There are high chances of these higher powers being misused, hence remaining surrendered at the feet of a guru during this sadhana is important.)

Another way of establishing such a supernatural state is to completely surrender oneself at the feet of a yogi or an enlightened guru and follow his gyana and sadhana. He himself always remains merged with the pure consciousness and has the power to merge us too in the same.

A guru is one who can give his own state to his

surrendered disciple at his free will. He has the power to create another of himself.

There is a famous couplet:

'Paras aru Guru me bahu antaro jaan,
voh loha kanchan kare, ye kare aap samaan.'

The paras, or touchstone, can only convert iron into gold but a
guru can elevate an ordinary person to become like himself.
Paras cannot make another paras but a guru can.

If we wish to transcend our physical finite limitations to infinite consciousness and become the master of the universe, the easiest way is to surrender at the feet of an enlightened guru. It is extremely difficult to go through the intense spiritual practices on one's own, especially while living in a family and performing all the worldly duties. However, if the guru's grace is bestowed upon us then an ordinary person can become extraordinary, and the finite can become infinite.

NECTAR OF GYANA:

- Being successful in life is our birth right. We just have to know the techniques to invoke our higher potential powers.
- Either you control life situations or else life situations will control your life. The choice is yours.

- The mind is the spark of consciousness and hence carries all the creative powers of the cosmic forces within it. Learn to tap them.
- Make daily positive affirmations, visualize your goals, seek forgiveness, meditate, and remain peaceful so as to tap the maximum of your subconscious mind.
- We can easily transcend the limitations of our body and become the infinite if we can surrender ourselves at the feet of a guru.

Unleashing Potential

During my youth I was a person without any special qualities or any major achievements to my credit, whether in academics or extracurricular activities. I had no particular passion, no hobbies, and an average IQ and EQ. I had no interest in academics or sports or art, nor did I have any goal in life. My only good quality was my behaviour, which was very cordial and comforting to everyone.

Since I had no goal in life, I was neither serious about my career nor helpful to my father in his business. My parents had only one opinion about me, and that was: good for nothing. This was exactly what my father once said to one of his friends while introducing me. He said, "This is my son and he is good for nothing! He comes to the factory just to pass his time!"

I would never forget those words. I walked away at the time, visibly embarrassed, without uttering a word. What was worse, I knew my father was not wrong. My college days were mostly spent in the carefree company of friends, which is typical of that age. But what bothered my father the most was that the same lethargic attitude lingered even after I had joined his business.

This embarrassing statement from my father was a turning point in my life. While it is possible that such statements from parents can lead to friction between parents and children, or the child going into depression or running away from home, or the child's increased negative behaviour and attitude towards life, it is also possible for exceptional people to take these negative statements as a challenge to prove themselves and their potential. Most people are not aware of their hidden potential, and this gets triggered sometimes either by life situations or the negative or positive comments made by people. Usually these comments, when made by a near and dear one, are to trigger that hidden potential, but are generally taken otherwise.

When someone says you cannot do something, there can be five types of reactions:

1. Agree that it's not in your destiny, hence you cannot do it and keep quiet.
2. Agree that your potential is limited because of a manufacturing defect in you and that you are a hopeless product.

3. Take it negatively and get disappointed, depressed, and resentful of the person who makes such comment.
4. Use the comment as an excuse to reinforce negative affirmations that you are good for nothing, that you cannot do anything worthwhile in life, that you are a failure, that no one likes or loves you, and that you are not a good decision maker or implementer. Basically, make yourself believe that you are devoid of any good quality.
5. Take the negative comment as a challenge and say to yourself that you can do it, that you will prove to yourself and others that you are an achiever and next time you will force others to reverse their opinion about you.

I reacted in the fifth way. I took it as a challenge and decided to prove to everyone that I am a capable person and I too can be an achiever. I worked hard and smart and started doing things differently. My positive behaviour came to my rescue, I started moving among successful people and I started visualizing big goals for myself. In a short period of time I was being recognized as a force to reckon with. I became the youngest president of the All India Association of my industry at the age of twenty-seven and was also conferred with 'Outstanding Entrepreneur of the Year' award. I became a picture of perfection, the man of the moment, a visionary, and a great speaker.

Once there was a person who did not work and lived on his wife's income. He was an alcoholic and remained drunk all the time. He was habituated to smoking, gambling, and fighting with his wife and both his sons. As his sons grew up, one of them became exactly like the father and the second one, having earned lot of money and respect, became a successful businessman.

One day a journalist asked both the sons who was behind what they had made of themselves. Both of them had the same answer—their father. The son who became useless like his father said, "Seeing my father doing nothing, I also became like him." And the successful son said, "Seeing my father doing nothing, I decided to do something extraordinary and not end up like him."

Two sons, having been brought up in the same atmosphere by the same parents in the same fashion, designed their destinies differently. One became a replica of his father and the second became the exact opposite.

Most of us blame our parents, the atmosphere at home, insufficient resources or fate and destiny for our failures and non-performance, but do not take the blame on ourselves. We do not realize that our destiny is in our own hands. We do not realize that whatever state we are in is the result of our past karma and that our present karma, our purushartha, the present effort, will decide and design our future.

Once when I wanted my father to give me more responsibilities and a greater role in our family business, he said, "If you are expecting me to give you some work and hand you over some responsibilities, that is not possible. Responsibility can never be given in charity. One must be capable enough to diplomatically take it from others and prove one's potential and that is the only way to grow and be a leader."

A leader is not he who does only what is expected of him, but he who exceeds the expectations of others. A leader is he who thinks differently and looks at things from a different perspective than others. A leader is he who might work hard but surely works smart. Hard work pays to the extent that the effort is put in, but smart work pays thousand times more than hard work.

When you work smart, you not only use your own potential to the fullest but also the potential of others and the potential of the cosmos. Physical potential is limited but mental potential is unlimited and immeasurable. Our mind is an extension of the cosmos and has all the powers of cosmos. Our brain's intellect is limited but the mind's powers are unlimited. When the mind's frequency is matched with the cosmic frequency, it draws upon the infinite potential of the cosmos.

This can be done by acknowledging and surrendering to the cosmic forces. Know that we are part of the cosmos and sent to the world to perform and achieve some of its goals and objectives, and that we will be extensively supported by it. Make the cosmos your boss, the master, the consultant, and the parent and witness its creative forces work for you.

Another major quality of a leader is that he makes everyone work the way he wants them to work but makes them feel that they have worked the way they wanted to work. Everyone works precisely as per the script of the leader but his script remains invisible to others.

A leader takes everyone along. He understands that if one wants to run the race fast, he runs alone but if he wants to run the race long he must run with others.

A leader is brave enough to take the blame for all the wrong decisions, failures, losses, unfavourable results and adversities, but at the same time is confident enough to give credit to others for right decisions and favourable results.

A person who enjoys the efforts he puts in the process, enjoys the fruit or results of those efforts too.

When our effort is only 50% of what we could've put in, then the result also will be 50% of what we could have got. If we are stressed while making the effort then the result might be stressful too. If the effort is joyful then the result of that effort will definitely be joyful.

For a successful person it doesn't matter whether the result of his effort has been favourable or unfavourable as his happiness or joy is not dependent upon the result but on the effort. Having enjoyed the effort, he has automatically enjoyed the result or the purpose of his effort too, as the result too would have just given him the same enjoyment and happiness. Hence, a successful person doesn't wait for the result of his effort to give him joy and happiness. He takes his pleasure in the process itself. His enjoyment is not in reaching some particular destination, but in the journey itself.

Being joyful, happy, elated, excited, energetic, and motivated is our free will. We can't buy these emotions from the market and they are not available in the grand bazaar. Even if we feel excited or motivated by reading a book or listening to a motivational speaker, still the excitement and motivation invoked comes purely from within. The elation was within us and through our own free will we invoke it.

No motivator can go inside us and awaken our potential. It's purely our free will to do that and the proof for this concept is that in the same motivational workshop some participants get motivated and others don't.

It is like the case of hypnotism, which is not possible without the consent of the subject (audience). Unless a person is ready to get hypnotized no hypnotist can put him under his spell.

Lord Krishna gave the same knowledge to Arjuna and Duryodhana but Duryodhana did not accept it and even Lord Krishna couldn't forcibly sow the knowledge in his mind.

In fact, Duryodhana at one point of time confessed to Lord Krishna that he himself knew that he was on the wrong side, on the side of adharma and unrighteousness, and requested Krishna to change his mind itself to absorb the truth instead of giving a discourse on what is right and what is wrong. To this Krishna said, *"I can only give gyana but you yourself have to accept that gyana and absorb it. I have no power to force upon anyone the truth or gyana which I give."*

This is the power of free will we possess which is even acknowledged by the gods.

In a school classroom there are say thirty students. All of them are taught by the same teachers throughout the year but at the end of the year different students fare differently. They all get different marks and grades in their studies.

What is the reason for this difference? Were the teachers biased? Did the teachers teach each student differently?

No, it was the free will of the students to learn and focus on what teachers taught. Everyone's potential is the same, except for very few who have some sort of physical or mental disability. The senses, mind, intellect, memory, etc., are the same in every soul. God has not created anyone with special love or vengeance. God is unbiased. It's only that some have invoked their potential by using their free will and others have not.

Everyone is blessed with the free will to empower themselves in any area or subject of their choice or in all them, if they choose to.

Once God appeared before one of his disciples and asked, "What do you want?" The disciple said, "Please give me truckloads of money, a mansion, imported cars, success in business, name, fame, a good spouse, and lifelong happiness."

God said, "My dear friend! I do not sell fruits, but I sell seeds. I will give you the seeds and you have to plant them in the soil of your mind, nurture them with care, and grow them into trees as big as you want."

God further said, "Whatever you grow in your mind I will manifest them in the gross world. Mind is your medium of communication with me. Whatever your mind signals, I give you that. Unfortunately, most of the time you have been sending me wrong signals. You've been sending me signals for things that you never wanted and when I gave you all that, you blamed me for it in return."

God's duty is to fulfil his subjects' wishes. He doesn't differentiate between what is good for us and what is not unless we are surrendered to him. He just gives us what we sow in our mind, as that is what signals our wishes to God. But most of us send confusing signals to God about our true desires as we have no control over our minds. Our minds are confused, unstable, negative, disorganized, unfocused, and jumbled with ideas and desires. In fact, most of the time we think more about what we don't want and less about what we want.

Consider the four states of a car:

1. The car is parked in the garage. Neither the engine is running nor are the wheels moving.
2. At the traffic signal or at a traffic jam, the engine of the car is on but the wheels are not moving.
3. The car is on the road and both the engine and the wheels are running.
4. While driving, there comes a downward slope and the engine is shut off but the car continues to cruise ahead.

These four states of a car can be compared to four states of human beings.

The first state, where both the car and engine are not in motion, can be compared to either the state of deep sleep or deep meditation. In both the cases we continue to exist and are not drained of our energies. Our energies are conserved in this state for future use. Wear and tear of the body and the mind, both are at a minimum.

The second state, where its engine is on but the wheels are not moving, can be compared to our state wherein we are thinking, getting worried, anxious, fearful, while sitting in one place. All our energies are drained out in this stage due to negative thinking.

The third state of the car, where the car is moving and the engine also is on, can be compared to the state wherein we are working and applying our intellect to the extent required at that moment for the work we are doing or for accomplishing a particular goal or objective.

The last state of the car, where the engine is turned off but the car is moving, can be compared to the state wherein we are working, moving, performing our duties and responsibilities, taking care of everything required, yet remaining in a state of complete peace and calm. We are not worried about the future, have no regrets of the past and are focused on what we want in the present. We are single-mindedly connected to the cosmos and see the cosmic forces working on our behalf.

This fourth state is the best state and every human being must aspire to it. The second state is the worst state where the mind is actively and excessively thinking and worrying, and is anxious and fearful. In this state we achieve nothing, yet consume all the available resources.

Most people fall under this second category. They achieve nothing great but blame others for their failures and fate. They come into this world, live, enjoy, crib, and depart without anyone recognizing their existence. Their coming into this world and exiting goes unnoticed.

Having come into this world we should utilize the opportunity to its greatest potential. We must achieve that for which we are sent to this world. We should tap the potential of the cosmos, available equally to everyone without any discrimination, to its fullest extent.

NECTAR OF GYANA:

- Smart work is the key to successful living.
- Be effort-oriented and not result-oriented.
- Learn to tap the enormous potential powers of the cosmos to achieve your goals. Know that nothing is impossible for the cosmic forces as they are the creators of the universe.
- Know that the feelings you invest into your effort will be reflected in the results too. If you are stressed during your effort your result too will be stressful and if you are joyful during your effort your result too will be joyful.
- Be a leader. Take the blame on yourself for everything that goes wrong and give credit to others for everything that goes right.
- We always have a choice to choose the path which may seem a little difficult but will eventually lead to success. Use your free will.
- God has already given us the seeds of success and happiness, we only have to nurture them.

A Mystic Guru

The occasion was my sister's wedding, which was to be held at Ladnun, our ancestral village in remote Rajasthan.

I had accompanied my father to invite Mamaji (Rajendra Brahmachariji, a yogi and my first guru) for the wedding. But Mamaji who was already on the path of spirituality and monkhood by then was not inclined to attend social events like weddings.

People who are involved in yogic sadhana try to reduce their socializing to a bare minimum to avoid any distraction. It's usually advised to all spiritual aspirants to reduce their socializing, meeting and mingling with people unnecessarily, to avoid talking or reading about any subject other than the spiritual subject, to avoid all those actions that can cause the mind to drift away from the spiritual subject, to avoid watching TV or movies which have excessive violence, or which awaken sleeping senses.

In any case Mamaji did not want to disappoint us and said that he will try to come.

It was summer and on the wedding day it started raining heavily unexpectedly, so much so that my parents feared that it would hinder the wedding. Ladnun being a small village was not equipped to handle any havoc created by incessant rain. But, strangely and suddenly, the rain stopped just before the arrival of the baraat, a procession in which bridegroom arrives for the wedding along with his parents, relatives, and friends. The marriage went smoothly without any hitch, much to everyone's relief.

On our return after the wedding, when I, along with my parents visited Mamaji, my father asked him why he hadn't attended the wedding. Mamaji was silent for some time and then he looked at my father, smiled and said quietly, "Who do you think stopped the rain?"

This one incident was very impactful to everyone's mind including mine. I was in awe of Mamaji and astounded to think that he had such powers that he could command nature to act in one way or the other to protect his disciples.

This was my first encounter with a yogi who seemed to have invoked higher potential powers beyond the 10% available to normal human beings.

Many yogis have acquired such miraculous and supernatural powers through their yogic sadhana especially through the awakening of their kundalini shakti. Kundalini shakti is the energy which normally lies dormant at the base of our spinal cord, known in Yoga Shastras as mooladhara chakra.

There are totally six chakras in the spinal cord, called shat chakras. These shat chakras are placed in a spiritual nadi (an invisible spiritual vein) called sushumna nadi. Special breathing techniques, yogic kriyas, and special meditation techniques are supposed to influence the flow of prana within this nadi and awaken the dormant kundalini shakti. Once this kundalini shakti awakens it starts piercing through these six chakras and as it pierces through each chakra, it endows the yogi with supernatural miraculous powers.

Supernatural powers—shaktis and siddhis—is the one thing which fascinates everyone. We believe in God only though the supernatural powers and not by any other attributes. If these supernatural powers were missing, then even God will not be considered as God.

Seeing Mamaji's powers there arose in me a strong desire to acquire such supernatural powers too. I was fascinated by the thought that I would be known world over for these powers and that I will be able to help people solve their life problems.

***

Like a bolt from the blue, an involuntary choice, a strong storm, the guru sweeps you off your feet to bring you back on the true path.

During one of Mamaji's subsequent visits to our home, he was sitting on a sofa with his white cloth under him in a padmasana. A few followers were sitting on the floor listening to him. Mamaji signalled me to come and sit next to him.

When I went over, Mamaji calmly looked at me and said in a matter of fact way, "I am going to give you a mantra that you must chant every day and you should start doing pranayama from tomorrow."

He whispered the mantra in my ears. I could not comprehend it in the first instance. Mamaji repeated the mantra a second and a third time and then asked me to repeat the mantra in his ears. I did as I was told and then looked into Mamaji's eyes for a moment. The eye-to-eye contact bewildered me as an involuntary shiver ran down the entire length of my spine. I did not understand what was happening. There was strong current flowing up and down my spine with intermittent jerks. This was my first experience of the flow of spiritual energy in my sushumna nadi, of which I had hitherto only heard of from Mamaji.

The guru was present. The shishya was present. The sacred mantra deeksha was passed on from the guru to the shishya. The entire cosmos was conspiring to bind them in this new bond. Shaktipat took place.

Shaktipat is the term used when a guru transfers his spiritual powers to his shishya through a mantra.

I chanted the mantra and, as the tongue wrapped itself around the words from an unaccustomed language and the mind darted back and forth with its sounds, the soul simply opened to a completely new, yet surprisingly familiar, world.

My eyes, which I had lowered in respect, now looked

up at Mamaji, the giver and now, the guru. As I received the mantra deeksha, the guru mantra, I did a shashtang namashkar (prostration) before my guru. I fell at his feet, touched my forehead to his toes, and, to my own surprise, my eyes started shedding tears of joy. I had never ever cried in my lifetime and I used to laugh at those who cried, either in ecstasy or in pain, thinking of them as weak. But that day was different. I had for the first time known the joy of crying.

I became acutely aware of my body reacting to the new stimuli. I could feel the hair stand on the back of my neck and goose bumps break out on my arms. An involuntary shiver ran down my spine and made me feel cold. In the very next moment I broke into a sweat, shedding away the weight of karma along with it.

Everything and everybody began to blur in my vision and I did not even notice when other people left the room. The stunned silence on my lips and eyes stood in stark contrast with the loud chants in my head. I closed my eyes and felt every little inner sensation.

The mantra reverberated and echoed in my eardrums louder and louder and gradually I felt as if every cell of my body was chanting that mantra. I also felt like I was hearing the same mantra from outside, as if it was being played on some distant loudspeaker. I couldn't understand what was happening to me and around me. Suddenly I felt a warm touch on my forehead and when I looked up I saw Mamaji touching my forehead with his soft palms and smiling at me, conveying at a glance that he understood what I was going through in that moment.

When the five physical senses reached their limits, I went beyond them into a new realm of experiences. Each word of the mantra seemed to open deep-lying knots whose existence I had not known till now.

As each knot opened something indescribable, a force, an energy was released in my mind. I felt as though a great weight had been lifted and there was an amazing sense of lightness. In a moment I felt like my mind had opened up from the top and was sending up some signal to the sky. This intense reverse lightning from head to sky drained me of every particle of energy. Shivers ran through me, every wave making me lose more and more consciousness of the world around me.

The waves travelled back and forth from the sky to the soul through the spine. Energy surged upward in a flow from the bottom of the spine, jerking the body, shaking it out of its current existential truth. As this energy travelled up and down several times, it gave birth to a sensation of bliss, a height of bliss and serenity such as I had never before experienced.

I sat living the experience and, one day not much later from this day, I would know that I had been bestowed with what was the kundalini awakening. The coiled primal energy which was sleeping at the base of the spine had got uncoiled and had awakened for the ultimate spiritual enlightenment.

The lightning that I had experienced shooting out of my head settled down in the space between the eyebrows on the agnya chakra, the third eye. This is the chakra that is empowered with mantra repetitions, the eye that is needed to see all that the other two cannot see.

The physical body could only bring forth streams of joyful tears when I regained consciousness. With moist eyes and a grateful soul, I prostrated once again at the feet of my guru in complete surrender. Whether it is joy or sorrow, an unbearable experience takes time to seep into one's existence.

I got up and quietly left the room. I lay on my bed with my eyes open, lost in a void. I was in a trance, stunned at the enormity of the situation which had shifted the paradigm of my world. Slowly, my eyes closed, and I fell asleep. I was on a different plane altogether.

I was deep in sleep and yet I was not sleeping. It was as if I was awake and yet I was asleep.

NECTAR OF GYANA:

- When a guru gives mantra deeksha, he transfers his spiritual powers with that mantra so as to clear our path for the spiritual journey.
- Guru means the remover of darkness. One who removes the darkness of our ignorance is a guru. They are lucky souls who have a guru in their lives.
- Surrender at the feet of a guru and seek his blessings. Even without making us go through the tortuous process of sadhana a guru can straightaway raise us to a higher plane which would otherwise have taken thousands of births to achieve.

Trial by Yogic Fire

The face beams looking up at the warm sunshine, belying the pain felt by the bare feet walking on thorns.

My mind had been under a kind of spell since the uttering of the mantra. Dedicated to the path unquestioningly, I took every opportunity to be of service to my guru, Mamaji. My only desire was to be in the presence of the man by whose grace I was on the speed lane of spirituality. An opportunity that I had never sought had not only presented itself to me but had even fallen right into my lap. The path, which the guru had nudged and prodded me into, now seemed to define my life purpose.

"Today you do the massage," instructed Mamaji.

I had hitherto only seen my cousin perform the very elaborate head massage. It was a ritual that Mamaji enjoyed after his deep meditation and yogic sadhana every day. I rubbed oil into Mamaji's scalp and with that began a new act in guru-shishya relationship that of guru sewa—service to the guru.

Besides the direct benefits of his blessings and the intensity of his meditation, there were numerous encounters like this wherein I unknowingly received the spiritual energy of the guru through sparsh (touch). Much like the earlier energy that I had received through the mantra deeksha where words unlocked internal energies and helped me in my spiritual evolution.

A guru does shaktipat—transfer of his spiritual powers to his disciples—through several methods. Some of the more common ones are:

Sound—through a mantra, through discourse, through bhajan, through calling of one's name, through the repetition of God's name, etc.

Touch—through a touch on the forehead, through applying a tilak at the agnya chakra, by patting the disciple's back as a form of blessing, through the massage of his head or toes, or by any other means through which he touches his disciple or allows the disciple to touch him.

Eyes—through eye contact with the disciple, whereby the spiritual light emanated from the eyes of the guru can invoke his disciple's spiritual powers.

Bhavana (Emotions)—While the former three methods require the physical presence of disciple in the proximity of the guru, a guru intending to do shaktipat can do so through bhavana even when the disciple is far away.

Shaktipat is done only to a disciple who has surrendered to the guru and is ready to receive higher spiritual energies, as otherwise if the disciple is not able to sustain that higher energy, it could cause physical or mental havoc for the disciple. It is akin to passing 440 volts of electrical current for an apparatus which is meant to operate only at 210 volts. The higher current will only damage the apparatus, not make it perform more efficiently.

We must never force the guru to do shaktipat and should leave it to him to decide when and how he wants to help us evolve spiritually. He knows best what suits us, when it suits us, how much suits us, and in what circumstances it suits us. We should just remain surrendered at the feet of the guru. Our sadhana (effort) is nothing more than surrendering our ego at the guru's feet, everything else is guru kripa (guru's grace).

***

Starting with my initiation, I had begun to practice yogic sadhana under Mamaji's guidance. Chosen by the guru, I was an initiated student.

Meditation was not easy. Neither was easy sitting in one posture for a long duration. I didn't know which was tougher. Sitting in padmasana for long stretches of time, which I wasn't used to, or trying to make my mind still, which seemed next to impossible. At times it would be overwhelming. But I had begun to contain myself extremely well.

"The mind is like a monkey. It keeps jumping from

one tree to another. One monkey is noise, two monkeys are cacophony, but hundreds of monkeys? It's an orchestra that is badly orchestrated. You should learn to bait the monkeys and make them listen to you. Only then will you be able to control your mind." Mamaji's words echoed in my ears as I tried to control the sea of thoughts I had crept into. Added to this were the various physical yogas, kriyas, mudras, and bhandhas which Mamaji made me do incessantly.

The easiest thing, by far, was following the prescribed diet, which was essential to achieve the maximum benefits from the sadhana. I was told to drink more than two litres of hot and salty water in one gulp. "It is called kunjal kriya," said Mamaji. *It is done to cleanse the system, to enable you to do better meditation, better pranayama. Your food pipe, air pipe, and internals must be as clean as a flute. Your body is a medium, we need to use it well.*

Another day Mamaji made me do dhouti kriya. "This five-metre cloth soaked in hot salty water should be swallowed until a small strip at the end is left to hold near your mouth. Then drink the whole two litres of hot salty water and vomit it out with the cloth. This cloth will flush out all the phlegm and impurities from the food pipe and stomach. A yogi's body has to be free from phlegm, acids, mucus, etc., for extended pranayama and meditation," said Mamaji.

After these kriyas I was able to hold my breath from thirty seconds to almost ten minutes at a time, in a practice called kumbhaka. When my breath was held inside me for so long I could feel my antar swas—internal breathing—taking place. I had heard about internal breath but never really understood what it was.

How do we feel during internal breathing? I could clearly feel my breath, slow and steady, from my abdomen to my throat and in reverse direction, without inhalation and exhalation through the nostrils. Up and down, down and up. There was no air getting out of nostrils nor coming in through nostrils. It was a fantastic feeling beyond description. I felt blissful witnessing this internal breathing and later on realized that it was a kind of meditation too.

Focusing on and enjoying this internal breathing I would also lose consciousness of time and space and the mind would become completely free of thoughts.

Pranayama means giving rest to prana. 'Prana' is the Life Force and 'ayama' means extension or to give rest, hence a breathing technique which reduces the inflow and outflow of breathing, elongates each breath, and holds the breath for long is real pranayama.

As per Yoga Shastras, our life span depends on how many breaths we take per minute or per day as, it is believed, when we are born we are born with a fixed number of breaths and not fixed number of years. How fast or how slowly we consume the breaths allotted to us at the time of birth decides how many years we will live.

This is true not only of humans but also of other living creatures. If we observe the breathing pattern of other living creatures we can see that a dog breathes fast, hence it's life span is less, whereas a crocodile breathes slowly, hence lives long.

When we get angry, anxious, irritated, or fearful our breathing becomes fast and ragged, and we consume the breaths available to us quickly thus reducing our life span. Breathing at a high rate under negativity is killing us slowly. It's slow poison and slow suicide. But when we are peaceful, relaxed, and meditative, our breathing slows down thus increasing our life span.

Most of our diseases also are related to our breathing pattern because breathing has a direct relationship to the state of the mind as well as to the functioning of internal organs. *Disease is nothing but dis-ease.* When the body and mind are not at ease they fall sick.

In Yoga Shastras, the remedy for many diseases is given through controlled and rhythmic breathing. Slow breathing helps control anger, anxiety, stress, tension, irritation, and other negativities.

Regular practitioners of meditation experience slow breathing during their meditation and almost zero breathing in deep meditation, during which time they lose body consciousness. We can control our breathing through either pranayama or through meditation. Both ensure a healthy body, healthy mind, and long life.

After regular practice of kriyas and pranayama, my meditation too became easier and effortless. I went beyond the limitations of a fixed time, fixed place, and fixed way of meditation. My meditation broke all boundaries and became boundless. It was then that I started realizing what meditation really meant.

Meditation is not about focusing or concentrating on an object or a sound. Meditation is just *being. Being our own Self. Being in the moment.*

Meditation is a state of being, a state of witnessing, a state of awareness. Being in the self without identifying with the modifications of the mind is a state of meditation.

Meditation is not mere concentration, though concentration could be a medium to progress in meditation and eventually establish one in meditation. Knowledge of the ultimate being, contemplation, and concentration could help one establishing oneself in a state of meditation. Through meditation, one realizes one's true nature of being the self, the atman, brahmanda, or pure consciousness— of merging with the eternal formless divine being.

Some refer to meditation as 'the effort put in to know the knower', some call it 'the result of effort put in to know the knower', and some even call it 'a journey from the known to the unknown'.

Meditation breaks the barrier of multiplicity, variety, and duality in creation. Through meditation 'many' become 'one' and 'one' becomes 'none'. Meditation is the source of joy, peace, contentment, and bliss. It also acts as a protective shield and protects us from others' negative vibratory influences.

Meditation removes illusions and delusions and casts aside the veil of maya from the divine existence of self, the atman. It allows the divine light of the Supreme Divine Being to encompass us and make us 'consciously conscious of our own consciousness'.

I realized this state myself during one of my trips to the famous temple of Badrinath in the Himalayas. Outside the temple were statues of various saints, including Shankaracharya. I carefully chose a place among them to meditate. In the chill winter of the high mountains, I felt no cold or discomfort and sat there for a long time, unmindful of the surroundings and people moving around.

At one point I became aware of a small group of tourists who had come to visit the temple and were looking at the row of statues. A young girl in the group said, "Look, that statue with white clothes and shawl is so life-like, so nicely made."

"That is not a statute, it is a person, I think," replied an adult.

"That is impossible, we have been here sitting for so long now and I haven't seen even the slightest movement in it," the girl insisted strongly.

As the family continued to discuss this further, their voices faded, and I felt pride warming my chest. I smiled internally without it reaching my lips.

The restless storms that had earlier stirred my soul had now calmed down. The yogic obsession had taken over my being and I only wanted to delve deeper.

In such a deep state of meditation, I experienced internal smells, sights and sounds that had begun to appear during my meditations. The chakras, or energy centres, present in the sushumna nadi within the spinal cord are normally blocked. But through the practice of intense yogic sadhana, these energy centres are opened up by the pressure of the prana, or life force. As they open up, they emanate various sights, sounds, and smells. Thus, I could experience the fragrance of sandalwood, the sound of a beating drum, a ringing temple bell, the music of a flute and sometimes Sanskrit shlokas would echo in my ears and lights of different colours and sometimes bright lightning would appear at the agnya chakra.

The antenna which was latent had become active to receive whatever the universe wanted to give and share. It was a reward I had never expected.

This internal awakening was insulated from the external life I led. Like a warm glow I carried it and was led by it.

NECTAR OF GYANA:

- Regulate your breathing through regular practice of pranayama for a dis-ease-free mind and body, and a healthy soul
- The best way to establish oneself in meditation is through meditation itself. Meditate regularly for peaceful living and for your spiritual growth.
- Witnessing thoughts during meditation and creating separation of our Self from the physical body makes us realize our true existence as the divine Self.
- Consciously be conscious of your own consciousness; the reality of life is consciousness and not worldly objects.

Meditator vs. Mediator

Descending the treacherous mountain was a long and tortuous ordeal. The rider braved it all—the hunger, the thirst, the rains, and the thunderstorms. Days and nights merged into one endless journey.

Finally the rider rejoiced to see a vast blue ocean ahead of him. The soothing waters beckoned his battered body. The waves lapped at his feet as he watched the distant sunset.

Suddenly an oyster brushed against his feet in the water. He gently picked it up and as a reflex to the touch, the oyster shed a tear.

To the rider's amazement, the tear immediately transformed into a shiny white pearl!

The rider smiled. He smiled in understanding . . .

Regular meditators who tread the path of spirituality and are simultaneously active in their worldly chores go through a division in their minds. One half remains the old dynamic personality who is a doer and a decision-maker, and the second one is this new self, the meditator, who is calm, composed, detached and a non-doer.

"Meditation is not meant for the meditator and meditator is not meditating. Meditation is meant to tame the mediator, the mind, whose nature is to focus on everything other than its own self."

I was beginning to understand the deep meaning of the above statement. We as the self, formless consciousness, are always in meditation. It's only the mind, who is the mediator between the individual self and the omnipresent self, that requires meditation so as to become peaceful and realize the link between the two selves.

The mind's nature is to always be in the thinking mode and focus on the external world by allowing all the five senses to remain engrossed in their subjects. This phenomenon creates a veil over the self. The self gets hidden under this veil and only through intense meditation is this veil lifted and the true self revealed. When the self is revealed, a state of duality comes into existence. One, the mind that is connected to world and the other, the consciousness that is connected to the divine self, pure and peaceful.

In the initial days, both would overlap without permission or a specific direction, making me appear like a dazed zombie at times and a hyperactive over-achiever at work at others, until I realized what was happening and consciously made efforts towards channelizing both.

At this stage the realization also dawned that we are not the normal human beings trying to seek and experience the divine being. We are actually the divine being, seeking the human experience. With this clarity, the way we live life and the purpose of life undergoes a 360-degree shift.

As we get accustomed to a regular regime of meditation, we start learning to switch one button on and the other one off depending on our need and requirement of the hour.

This is like taming a tiger and awakening the Buddha or putting the Buddha to sleep and allowing the tiger to hunt.

At times, this presents difficulties because of the tiger-like nature of the mind. It would just encompass the whole space in its incessant prowling. Likely because we have given the tiger free rein all our lives. The Buddha trait appears to be non-existent to us. Though it existed all along, making its presence felt in subtle and firm ways, we remain unaware of it.

It only takes some time for a seeker to realize that the dormant was after all not so dormant. What is required is to acknowledge its presence and become aware of it, for it to take on an active role in our lives. After the initial days of struggle, once we realize this, everything becomes a little easier to accomplish.

The over-achiever in us will start wanting more. Our mind will always ask for more and ask, 'What next?' even as we start experiencing the happiness for which we had been longing for millions of births.

Nectar of gyana:

- Consciousness, the self, is in reality the meditator and mind is the mediator and becomes the link between individual consciousness and the omnipresent consciousness.
- Know that we are actually divine being seeking human experience and not human beings seeking divine experience.

Transcending the Duality

Achievement brings pride; true understanding elevates you to the sky and makes achievement look like a distant mountain peak far below.

As always, when I started to meditate I did pranayama, chanting the mantra Mamaji had given me. Saying the verse repeatedly sent my mind into a trance and soon I didn't need the aid of the mantra. The mantra was just a spark needed to ignite the dormant energy already within me. My mind's eye turned inwards and began to gaze upon the infinity that existed within.

I sat for dhyana, ramrod straight, the body upright in padmasana, my fingers overlapping on my lap with the tips of the thumbs touching each other.

Thud. Once.

Thud. Thud. Twice and over and over again. My back hit the wall, I thought I was losing balance and inched away from the wall towards the centre of the room, so I could focus on meditation. The thumping against the wall stopped, the movements did not. I at first felt the sway, front and back, in the upper and lower parts of the body. My body felt the jerks, my mind refused to ponder on these sensations keeping the focus solely on meditation.

Over the next few days my meditation practice was always punctuated with the jerks. They had begun softly and increased in intensity. My head now jerked and shook vigorously, but I trained my mind to un-imagine any such realities.

As I continued in deep meditation, my arms slid open involuntarily. The jerks seemed to be caused by live wires carrying current throughout the body. I realized that the jerks were caused by my life force, my prana, entering the sukshma nadis, an internal intangible neural system existing in a different dimension.

These nadis which have no physiological presence are channels that exist for prana to move when it gets subtle. The dominant nadi that is in the middle of the spine is known as the sushumna nadi, a single pathway that is present from the head to the bottom of the spine. It is the main node in which nestle all the chakra, central to yogic practices. As I lingered my attention longer on these nadis I noticed that the energy flow was flowing with a set path. It was not just random acts or burst of energy, but a set path that energized different nodes as it travelled in purposeful paths. I could process all this knowledge conceptually only later in my spiritual path, but for now, my subtle experience was speaking volumes to me.

I had travelled deep within myself to enter the matrix of the spirit and travel amongst the software digits that controlled everything that the body experienced.

A revelation was of seeing the motherboard where all human experience was generated. I had hitherto experienced only that which my external sensory organs allowed, but now every experience of my inner being became instantly accessible to me.

These were smells, the sounds, and lightning experienced at a plane that no external eye, ear, or nose could fathom. At the pinnacle of this experience, I felt grateful to my guru, Mamaji, who, I was sure, was the enabler of all such experiences, accessible only to yogis.

I felt like a strain of soft pure gold in the hands of a skilled goldsmith who had beaten it sore to make it malleable to its flexible most. As my internal circuit lit up with the roving prana, I experienced a burst of joyful sensations, even while my body continued jerking. The jerks came slowly, initially, and occurred only once in a session of meditation. But soon the occurrence accelerated and began to occur multiple times in each session. I felt a tug-of-war between the prana wanting to reach its ultimate destination and the nature of the earth's gravity that pulled it towards the physical grosser realities.

At last the jerking stopped.

As prana made its presence felt in my head region, I began to feel ethereal. At the end of this manthan, this churning of life energy, my prana felt at its lightest. I had burned my fats, of the physical body and of the spirit by depleting karma, and my whole being felt lightweight.

With the prana reaching its destination, there was no more struggle and no need to count the minutes and hours that I sat in meditation. And one day, as naturally as vapour rises into the clouds, it happened.

With my knees folded in the meditating pose, it took me a few seconds to realize that I was a few feet above the ground involuntarily. My body was floating in air. I was levitating.

It happened when I did my part and left the rest to the forces of the cosmos. And the more I followed the path of prana, the easier it became to levitate, which I did over and over again.

Having thus surrendered to the path and to the guru, I wasn't even sure what or where was the end. I let the prana roam freely while completely enjoying each and every bit of this new learning. Hidden in the nooks and corners were titbits of information, some from past lives, some from the future of this life. I saw flashes that began to play out on a screen of a sublime theatre, the consciousness.

My body was at its lightest, my mind was at its highest. Even when I opened my eyes and touched the ground I experienced a sense of being above everything terrestrial. The physical act surprised me no more, and I was not eager to talk about it to anyone. It was like a deep conversation between me and the energies of the universe. I had chased this experience for a while now, but when it finally happened I wasn't thinking of the actual experience anymore.

Like every milestone in the yogic sadhana, every stage is a foundation for greater things to follow. Every experience is a door to a new room of more unexplored experiences. The physical act is a mere instrument to something increasingly sublime. I sensed inner peace like never before, a peace that bathed all sensation in and around me. The longer I persisted with these experiences the longer the peace lingered with me. The peace moved me to a state of inaction, where my mind did not seek or desire any action.

I dwelled in peace as my body learnt to levitate or stay afloat in space without any support. I understood now that it was my soul that was on a different plane, living a life of elevation.

NECTAR OF GYANA:

- Even though the body is made up of gross matter, it can still float in the air when the soul floats in the heart.
- Mysterious is the physical body and mysterious is the working of the prana. When the prana enters the mysterious sukshma nadi in the body, spiritual mysteries get revealed.
- Spiritual sadhana, meditation, and pranayama reveal the real hidden purpose of life. Life is given to us not just to get engrossed in the world, but to unravel the mysteries of life itself and to realize the higher being in the human being.

Astral Travel

One day Mamaji mentioned the sukshma sharira, which I had heard about on and off in the past, though my understanding of it was vague. Unable to contain my curiosity, I asked, "What is sukshma sharira, Mamaji?"

"Well, it is the soul that can engage in astral travel. My guru used to make astral travel at his free will through his sukshma sharira. His soul would get out of the body and make astral travel wherever he wished to and come back to the body whenever he wished so," said Mamaji.

"Mamaji, what is astral travel?" I asked. Again, it was something I had heard about but not really understood.

"The soul or the sukshma sharira coming out of the body and moving around independently in the space is called astral travel," Mamaji explained.

"What? But the soul comes out of the body only when we are dead, isn't it, Mamaji? Then how can the soul travel?" I asked, confused.

"It is possible. That is the whole trick. Through yogic practices one can experience the soul without the support of the physical body and without necessarily going through the path of death," Mamaji explained.

"Wow, Mamaji, that is amazing! But how is it possible?" I asked in complete astonishment.

"Through this very sadhana, the path that we are now following, but it cannot be done by anyone and everyone. Even among the rishis and sanyasis, only a few yogis have been able to get the soul out of the body and do astral travel," Mamaji said. "But the best part is the soul can travel anywhere it chooses to. The entire universe is at its disposal."

I listened, totally fascinated.

"But . . . but how does the soul travel, Mamaji? Is there a special vehicle or something?" I asked in the flow of the conversation without thinking.

Mamaji laughed uproariously. "I knew you were intelligent, but I didn't know that you were funny too. Vehicle? My God!"

"Mamaji, why is astral travel so important?"

"To realize the separateness of soul from the physical body and eventually to attain samadhi," said Mamaji.

"Samadhi? But Mamaji, samadhi means burying the dead body in the grave . . ." I trailed off in confusion.

"Samadhi is the ultimate goal for any yogi in the yogic sadhana," Mamaji responded, cryptically.

I took a minute to process what I was hearing. Finally I said, "Mamaji from what I have understood, astral travel means the soul going out of the body and travelling everywhere and samadhi means the ultimate internal realization of the soul. So where is the connection between the two? Why is astral travel required to achieve samadhi?"

"Do you remember in our previous discussion I mentioned that the soul can come out and do astral travel when a person is alive and not dead?" Mamaji said.

"Yes, I remember, Mamaji."

"Now tell me, what is that single most hindrance which stops a person's soul from coming out while he is alive?" Mamaji asked eagerly.

This time I was at a loss. I said sheepishly, "Mamaji, how would I know? I have not done astral travel."

"It is fear!" he said.

"Fear? Fear of what?" I asked.

"The fear of death, what else."

The realization struck me and I was totally amazed.

"Our fear of death is the major obstruction for the soul to come out. If one can transcend this fear, the soul can come out and do astral travel. And once the soul starts coming out, effortlessly overcoming this fear, only then will it continue its journey towards sahastrara, the final chakra in the middle of the head, and meet Shiva. Becoming one with Shiva is samadhi," Mamaji explained with much intensity and passion.

"My God! This is truly breathtaking, Mamaji."

"Literally and figuratively. That is the reason why astral

travel is so important. Why do you think I am struggling so much?" said Mamaji, sounding exhausted. "But remember, the paths one has to cross over time is truly a trial by fire. The soul knocks at the door over time but hesitates and is afraid to make the jump through the navel. Fear has to be overcome before the soul goes out of the body." He grew serious. "The preparedness and willingness to die joyfully if anything goes wrong is the price a yogi must pay. One must be ready to die in case the experiment fails, and there are many failures, I know some of them too well."

"I understand, Mamaji. But there is one basic question. If the soul can get out of the body and do astral travel by piercing through the chakras, why have you not been able to do it with your fifty years of sadhana, Mamaji?" For a moment I wondered whether I had crossed the line. "I mean, why is it that you are not able to pierce the chakras and go further and do astral travel?" I pushed on, boldly.

Mamaji was silent for some time, then finally said, "In all the things that we have discussed so far, there is one factor—the most crucial one—that I haven't told you about."

"What is it, Mamaji?" I asked.

"It is guru kripa, grace of a guru! Without this, it is very difficult to go ahead. Only with long practice and surrender at the feet of the guru can someone cross the threshold of fear. When the soul leaves the body, the body almost stops breathing, very much like death itself. It is not easy, but if there is sufficient support from the guru, especially at the time when the soul leaves the body, the disciple gets courage." He paused, as I hung on to his every word. "And it is my misfortune that my guru left his body before he could guide me in this and, at present, I am still unable to find a guru who can guide me. And that is the reason that I am still stuck at this stage and trying on my own," Mamaji said with a hint of sadness in his voice.

After a pause, he continued with a renewed spark in his eyes, "But, the magic of astral travel is such that *when a yogi successfully undertakes astral travel, he wins over the fear of death. One realizes the beauty of being without the physical body, the beauty of weightlessness, the beauty of being invisible yet seeing everyone and everything, the beauty of being independent and all alone in space and the beauty of being freed from needing food, water, shelter, or sleep. A free bird unmindful of rain, light, or darkness. No transactional tension of earning a livelihood and no duties and responsibilities."*

"Mamaji, I am fascinated by astral travel and I am eager to try it. Fortunately, I have my guru with me. And that is you. So, if you shower me with your grace and blessings, can I try it too?" I asked hesitatingly.

Mamaji's eyes opened wide in amusement. "Seriously! Here I am struggling to pierce through my own chakras and now you want to do astral travel. Wow!"

NECTAR OF GYANA:

- When we separate the soul from the physical body, we overcome the fear of death as we become aware that when death takes place, it is the death of the physical body and not of the soul.

- Samadhi basically means samadhan, which means clarity in totality. The clarity of our existence as soul, clarity of the manifestation of the physical world, clarity of the Supreme Divine Being and the individual being, clarity of space outside and inside, etc., is considered as samadhi, wherein there are no doubts left on any aspect of the creation.

- The ultimate stage in samadhi is sahaj samadhi, that is achieving a deep sleep state internally, while being fully awake externally. It is a state in which we can perform all the physical and mental duties in the world, and yet remain connected to the Supreme Divine Being.

The Mesmerising Master

One day one of my friends told me about a saint by the name of Sri Poornananda Swamy and insisted on my meeting him. He believed that this Swamiji was enlightened and had realized the ultimate truth, the self and the brahmanda.

"Interaction with him can open the knots of our minds in different ways and can help us go beyond the realm of our current awareness and understanding. It could lead to a complete change in perception of spiritual sadhana and help us in achieving enlightenment," said my friend.

"If I am destined to meet Swamiji, then surely I will meet him," I said to my friend, not showing much interest as I already had a guru and I had no thought of meeting anyone else for my spiritual pursuits.

"Okay," said my friend. "You know I read somewhere that one meets his destiny often on the road he takes to avoid it. So, you never know."

As things turned out, it wasn't long after this that I met Swamiji for the first time when he was visiting my city. He had a bright saffron tilak on his forehead that resembled the third eye, symbolizing the inner state of evolution. He wore a knee length saffron-coloured cloth and covered his chest with another unstitched saffron cloth.

There was a sense of divinity in his aura. His face was serene, and he was glowing. It was as if the source of light was within him and he was radiating light all around. He was still and composed and was in deep silence. But his very silence and the slight smile playing on his lips spoke volumes. His keen eyes seemed to penetrate every cell of our body, mind, and soul. It was difficult to look at him and even more difficult to make eye-to-eye contact.

He looked so pure, yet powerful, so pious, yet fearless. For a moment I felt as if I was seeing the most primal version of Lord Shiva himself. So raw, so potent, and yet so divine.

I could not believe that I could be so captivated and mesmerized by someone whom I had just seen. I was at such a loss of words that I could only stand and stare at him.

I was still staring at Swamiji when finally he looked directly at me. It was an intense, penetrating look. Immediately I felt a current pass through me and it was as if an invisible bond had formed between Swamiji and me.

I felt as if this was where I was meant to be. I felt like a lost child who had finally found his mother. It was as if I had found the entire universe in Swamiji's eyes and that one look was an answer to all my questions. Unaware of my own self, I finally tasted pure bliss which rolled down from my eyes as tears. I felt at home.

"Swamiji, I wish to seek your blessings. Please bless me and help me in my spiritual pursuits."

Swamiji smiled. He looked at me and said, "Definitely, my blessings are always with any person who is genuinely seeking the truth." Saying this he touched and rotated the ring finger of his right hand on my agnya chakra, the space in between the eyebrows, and blessed me.

***

"*Swamiji!*" I shouted as I woke up with a start. My heart was pounding, and I found myself sweating in the middle of the night. My breathing was heavier than usual, and it took me a moment to grasp my surroundings and come back to my senses.

I went and sat in silence on a chair by the window. It was a dream! I had figured that out by now. But what was surprising was the fact that I had seen a seer in my dream with an image of Shiva in the background. That seer in the orange robe was Swamiji. There was no doubt about it. But Shiva and Swamiji together?

But, how come? What is the connection? I had only met Swamiji once. I knew I was impressed by him. Actually, more impressed than I was willing to admit. I could not ignore how I had felt when I first saw Swamiji. But was I so impressed that he would start appearing in my dreams?

I got up and went to my meditation corner in the room and sat down. I sat down in padmasana and closed my eyes for meditation. Being a seasoned practitioner by now, my mind would usually immediately come under my control. But somehow this time, it kept wandering and suddenly Swamiji's face appeared before my eyes.

I wondered what was happening. Why was Swamiji appearing in my meditation? Determined to enter my usual meditative state, I again tried to concentrate as I knew these images of Swamiji were just my imagination as Swamiji himself could not enter my meditation.

But again, his face appeared. How can somebody impact me this much? I wondered again.

Not sure about what was happening I decided to bow down to Swamiji in meditation and seek his blessings and, to my wonder, I saw Swamiji smiling and blessing me with his hands touching my head. I was awestruck. I could actually feel the touch of his hands, the warmth of his palms, on my head. It was unbelievable.

This was undoubtedly an altogether new experience for me—feeling like I was in the physical proximity of someone who was, in reality, far away. And after a moment of confusion, I surrendered to the novelty and joy of the experience. During the course of my meditation, I heard Swamiji telling me to come to him at his Srisailam Ashram the next day.

The next day I went to the ashram. The lush greenery overlooked the surrounding hilly area. Everything was bright and colourfully decorated to celebrate Mahashivaratri. People were wishing one another, hugging and laughing. The young and old, dressed in vibrant hues had filled the large open space in the centre of the ashram.

If a group of young boys were dancing on one side of the space, on the other side an audience was enthralled by divine bhajans. People were also thronging the far end of the space, where there was a spread of delicious delicacies. Overall the otherwise quiet hermitage resembled nothing short of a colourful fair on the day that I entered it.

"My God! This place definitely doesn't look like an ashram," I exclaimed.

"It is organized this way because it is Swamiji's core belief to celebrate everything in life. And one need not be devoid of fun while being on the spiritual path. This ashram is an embodiment of everything he truly believes in," said one of Swamiji's disciples.

I couldn't help but find a contrast in Mamaji's and Swamiji's views.

One advocates spirituality sans celebration.

The other advocates spirituality through celebration.

Who is right? I was confused. Till now I had been thinking along the lines of Mamaji and of yogic sadhana where we needed to withdraw our senses from their subjects, control the mind, desist from any sort of entertainment, and eat in strict moderation.

When I was sitting beside Swamiji, one of his devotees

prostrated before him and sought his blessing on the special occasion of Mahashivaratri. He said "Swamiji, please bless me for the success of my worship of Lord Shiva. I have been fasting for the whole day today."

"You have been fasting?" asked Swamiji.

"Yes, Swamiji! As per the practice on Mahashivaratri, I am observing a fast and will only eat tomorrow morning after I complete all the rituals such as puja, mantra chanting, and shivalinga abhishek."

The devotee was obviously expecting appreciation from Swamiji for his strict adherence to rituals, but Swamiji responded, "If you are fasting then get out of my ashram. It's only feasting here, and not fasting, on Mahashivaratri." As the devotee looked on, stunned, Swamiji continued, "How can you think of God on an empty stomach? How can you feel emotionally connected to God when your stomach is crying for food? God cannot be happy seeing his devotees hungry just like parents cannot be happy seeing their children hungry. Moreover, since God resides in our hearts, the food that we eat goes directly to God only. When we are hungry we are keeping God hungry as well."

I was once again awestruck by such an answer from a saint, a sanyasi, who, in India, is supposed to strictly adhere to religious rituals and practices. I found Swamiji to be completely different from others. He appeared to be a revolutionary saint, unbothered by any criticism of breaking the traditional norms of sanyasa and religious rituals. He had to be highly evolved to be able to do this.

Somewhere in my heart, I felt a strong connection to Swamiji's approach as I too had never believed in religious rituals and God being bound by rituals. I too believed in a formless omnipresent God, residing in everyone's heart and residing everywhere in the universe in his omnipresent state.

After a while Swamiji looked at me, smiled, and said, "How was your meditation yesterday?"

I couldn't believe it. He seemed to know what had happened in my meditation the previous day. I had no answer.

He continued, "I am happy that you came today to my ashram on my invitation from yesterday. This proves your surrender and seriousness in pursuing spirituality. I had already blessed you when you met me first and yesterday too through your meditation."

I sat listening to Swamiji in amazement. I had never met anyone so evolved that he could enter my meditation and take control of my mind and bless me through meditation with the same effect as if it were in the real gross world.

Swamiji asked, "Are you interested in astral travel?"

I didn't reply as by now I realized that I was sitting before someone who knew everything, who had all the power to grant my wishes, and who could direct me to my ultimate spiritual destination. Here was an enlightened saint who could shower his grace on anyone who surrendered unconditionally to him. I prostrated before him.

"Tomorrow onwards your astral journey will start," said Swamiji, touching my head with his hands.

I felt the same feeling that I had felt the previous day during my meditation. Same palms, same warmth, same bliss.

NECTAR OF GYANA:

- The purpose of fasting during some religious occasions is to keep us away from the daily chores such as cooking, cleaning, and eating, so that we can remember God during the extra time available, but that seldom happens. Instead, if feasting and celebration give inner joy, then that inner joy itself is a connection to God.
- Surrender to and believe in the guru and experience the magic taking place in life. All the worldly as well as spiritual aspirations get fulfilled effortlessly without even speaking a word.
- Surrender to a guru means allowing him to take over our intellect, mind, and spiritual aspirations. He becomes the best judge to decide what to give, when to give, and how to give.

The Take-Off

During a journey, some see places, some gain experiences, and a lucky few find themselves. In the most intimate of journeys, we are united with the cosmos.

The urge to explore unchartered territories was both exciting and intimidating. I wanted to experience astral travel, even though I did not fully understand what it was or what was needed to do it.

I was sitting in meditation as usual when I felt an unpleasant knocking sensation at the navel.

My limbs jerked involuntarily as though a current was passing through them.

Thump, thump, thump.

My heart was on overdrive.

There was no physical injury on the navel but what I felt seemed a hundred times worse.

It felt a plethora of feelings and sensations that were beyond explanation. These sensations kept building up incessantly, till they reached a peak.

Then suddenly, everything—I mean *everything*—stopped. The world came to a standstill.

The jerking stopped.

The knocking stopped.

The palpitations stopped.

I was devoid of all feelings and nothing seemed to exist. It was as if somebody had pressed a pause button on my life.

And then I felt it. I could feel myself lift, defying gravity. I was floating.

I knew I was not just levitating because now I could feel no body weight, not even the nominal weight that I could during levitation. The feeling of sheer weightlessness was nothing short of pure bliss!

I saw nothing. I felt nothing. I was thinking of nothing. I was in supreme ecstasy!

There was a sense of being complete, of wanting nothing more.

The serenity and peace were beyond all human imagination. At this moment there was no imagination, no thought. Only the beautiful sensation of the soul, a distilled drop of bliss!

It permeated my entire being and I was drenched in this pool of euphoria where I did not seem to exist anymore.

Even before I could savour the moment fully, a

thought slowly made its way into my consciousness. Was there actually nothing to feel?

Had I died and hence lost all sensation?

Scary.

Thud!

With the occurrence of the thought, I lost the sensation of floating and returned to physical consciousness. My soul that had seemed to be drifting somewhere outside came back into my body.

Had I experienced the out-of-body experience? Did I really cross the threshold, and was it the fear for my life that brought me back?

Once again, I continued with more determination than ever before. "You have begun to achieve what you set out for," I told myself. "Today is the day you conquer fear."

I sat there for hours and hours together before I could feel nothingness, until I could stop trying to experience and let the nothingness set in.

I started floating and going in a certain direction but the pull at the navel was strong and it felt like I was at the very threshold and but unable to take the last step.

Thump . . . Thump . . . Thump, the constant noise was getting louder. It was so loud that I could feel it physically inside me. It seemed as though my abdomen was a woofer playing the heaviest of drums. Only, I didn't understand what the tune was or why my body was feeling these things that I had never felt before. My senses were failing me and I was losing comprehension of how I should perceive anything.

The pulse was racing, threatening to pop the veins in the forehead. My tongue felt dry and parched.

The breath was draining out of my body, taking all life force with it. The force was knocking hard at the navel that felt like it would give way any moment and burst open.

My heart beat hard like it was trying to escape the ribcage. The palpitations were out of range of any medical instrument. My sweat ran down in streams, soaking me. My body was jerking in all directions. All pain thresholds had been crossed, and the throbbing agony was making my mind numb.

It was a watershed moment. I was at the mercy of an extremely powerful energy that could not be reined in.

My body had earlier felt things that I had paid scant attention to. Now it seemed to come to a point that there would be nothing else.

But neither was I curious nor trying to comprehend the sensations; all I was trying to do was survive. My entire being was pulsating and seemed to be at a brink of some threshold. Life itself seemed to be draining out of me along with my breath. Yet I could not open my eyes; I sat completely still in sharp contrast to the inner tug-of-war going on inside me.

Finally I could not take it anymore. Was this the end? Would all the material achievements, the months of intense practice of this very difficult yogic sadhana, perish with my body?

Then, at the peak of this physical struggle and mental storm, came a sudden calm, a deafening silence and stillness that was scary in its own way.

And then it happened.

I stepped out of my body and saw my own body. It was me.

Me, exactly the way I see myself in the mirror. My eyes were closed.

Was I seeing myself from the outside? It was an intense second, but the sight was crystal-clear and unforgettable. There I was in space opposite my own physical body.

Was I out, was I in, was I alive, or was I dead?

If I just saw me, then who really was 'I'?

I felt that I had achieved the purpose of this lifetime, maybe many lifetimes. As if this was the journey that I had always intended to take and that all other journeys had led up to this road.

A milestone achieved! And what a show it was!

I saw 'Me'!

I looked at my physical body and felt like this was the first time I was seeing myself up close. I sat cross-legged in the padmasana posture, my eyes closed. In meditation, there wasn't even a single crease on my forehead. I was the very picture of serenity. Both my soles faced upwards towards the ceiling and my palms overlapped one another, with the tips of the thumbs touching each other. This vision of me sitting face to face with myself in meditation was a strong one.

Yet it was very brief, too brief to even measure in time. Unbelievably, here I was for the very first time outside myself. It was just for a fraction of second that I saw my body, a flash of a sight that is etched forever in my memory. The calm and serene expression of my physical body belied the turmoil that I had just experienced.

Even at the height of an elevated experience, the human creature has a narcissistic strain and wants to see itself first. Or is it the deepest desire of life to understand oneself which is at the core of all quests?

Beyond the realms of knowledge, my soul saw my body. Therein lay the knowledge that my soul knew—that the physical body and the soul are different entities. My physical body has merely been acquired by my soul in this birth.

It was an introduction at the astral level, where the soul acknowledged to a mind of its own that this was the physical body that it was associated with in this birth. Like it was marking the body as its residence address that it must return to in this lifetime no matter where it travels in the soul form.

Within the confines of an ordinary brick-and-mortar room, I had transcended the senses and the physical body in one of the most extraordinary experiences of my life.

My life has more than once presented circumstances where I have questioned who I really am, but not even in my wildest imagination had I looked at myself or the world around me in this manner. I could not decide if I was part of a grand illusion or if this was the reality and I had been living in the illusion all along.

Was this the magic of some twisted mind? Was I feeling empowered while I was actually a pawn in a plot I had no understanding of? For once I could travel as fast as my thoughts. It is an indescribable feeling to live a dream that I never dreamt.

The experience and these questions shook me and I opened my eyes. Everything was deceivingly as it was when I had sat down to meditate. By the time I learnt how this experience was defined, I had been through this travel several times. Each time, each day, lingering a bit longer outside myself.

I began to approach and look forward to meditation the same way a naughty child wishes to be left alone at home. This new body, the astral body, was my own yet it was all so new to me. I couldn't wait to explore. All the struggles I had gone through had in fact smoothened the path to this achievement.

All thresholds had been crossed after my first flash encounter with the image of myself. The astral body travelled outside the physical body for a little longer than a minute. The next time I persisted, and it seemed I could go out long enough to register everything around me.

Three times, four times, my astral body began to step out and stay out longer each time, for a few minutes at a time.

I had become comfortable with it now.

***

Every experience, however intense it might be, takes time to internalize. The travelling soul had made me feel like I was a sponge waiting to absorb so much from the universe. Perhaps that's why it took time for me to understand fully that the astral form was so powerful that it could see everything, yet not be seen.

Then it struck me—could I see the astral *me*, the soul? What did the subtle body look like without flesh and bones? Did it have any form at all?

I could not wait to find out. I exited the physical body in meditation and I went to my bedroom where there was a mirror. I stood in front of the mirror but couldn't see myself. Was I invisible? Is the soul invisible? The inquisitiveness to see myself as soul started growing in me.

During meditation I focused on this question and one day the answer was revealed to me.

It was revealed that when I leave the body, I should remain connected with the physical body. The physical body is connected to the soul through a string of invisible prana, just like a kite is connected to the person flying it through a thread. Though they both are two separate entities yet when both are in tandem and feeling the oneness, that's what will enhance the power of soul outside the body. There in the physical body, through the brain, I should concentrate on increasing the level of my soul consciousness with the required intensity while the soul is in front of the mirror.

I tried executing this thought once, twice, but didn't succeed. I persevered for a couple of days to keep the body, which was in meditation, and the soul, outside the body, connected in oneness.

One day after I successfully felt this oneness while being in front of the mirror, I tried to increase my consciousness in the meditating body as if I were increasing the regulator of a fan. As I used my mental faculties I realized that the mind is part of the soul. The soul is the astral body. Stepping outside the physical body the soul is free. In the body, it operates under the compulsions of the body and the brain but outside there are no parameters, no designs to adhere to. The cosmos is the limit.

With some effort and intense concentration simultaneously in the brain of the body and in the mind of the soul, I felt higher consciousness and suddenly, I saw a spark in the mirror. It lasted for just a flash of a second, but its presence was unmistakable.

The energy present in the soul is but the spark of consciousness. A part of the super consciousness present in the universe.

I continued this practice for some days and over some days I could see the spark of light continuously for some time. I realized that it was me as soul. It was a spark of bright light. Now I was in control of my soul and could keep it out of the body as long as I wanted and see it in the mirror also for as long as I wished.

I now aspired to increase my consciousness from a spark to a bigger size. I continued increasing my concentration in the meditative body to increase my consciousness and slowly I could increase the size of my soul. The amazement continued as I could also create shapes of my soul consciousness. These shapes which I could see in the mirror were not made up of solid matter but were of light.

Even as I played with cosmic light, I began to dwell on the play till I started to understand the nature of such light itself.

NECTAR OF GYANA:

- Know that we are the soul and not the physical body. The soul is a separate entity from the physical body and continues to remain alive with or without the physical body.
- Let the death of the physical body not create fear, as we as a soul will continue the journey even without a physical body.
- The soul is a spark of the omnipresent consciousness, the Supreme Divine Being, and it will eventually merge into its source after its enlightenment.
- The soul is the light. Realize this 'light' while being alive.
- The purpose of human birth is not just to remain engrossed in the physical matter of the physical world, but to realize the entity of our soul by using the vehicle of physical body.

Spirited Soulplay

My astral body stepped out of the physical body. I was now ready to move more purposefully outside my physical body and savour all the sensations at levels that were hitherto unknown to me. I wondered if I would need a door to leave the room. I began moving towards the wall or at least what seemed to be the wall. How fast was I going? As I got close to the wall, it didn't seem like a wall anymore, it didn't look like a solid block of mass either. Everything was a blur and out of focus.

There was space now between the walls! Like everything was moving away. But what was it that was moving away? The space increased and I felt like I was being swallowed into what seemed to be a forest.

A forest of what?

What were these things that seemed larger than me? Were they particles of the wall or were they atoms?

By moving away from my body had I become lost?

What was this place?

Should I go ahead, was it safe?

Mired in doubt, I collected all my powers and returned to the physical body.

Then I recollected Mamaji's words—nothing can be accomplished with fear. I reprimanded myself and came out of the body again.

All right, let me do this, which way should I take? Right or left?

Left. I went with my instinct.

There were particles that seemed suspended in air but connected in some way. These particles seemed larger than me; I felt I was suspended in this haze of matter.

There had to be a way out of this. I tried to follow the shape of the particle, but it was difficult to even know its shape when I couldn't see it in its entirety.

I could not say if I was going in circles or moving ahead along a path, or whether there was a path at all.

Was I going backwards from where I had started?

Where had I started?

Ah! The wall . . . the wall.

Am I still in the wall?

Why am I amused even when I can understand nothing?

As I passed through this endless loop, I tried to think of a way out.

If I could not penetrate a six-inch wall, how could I imagine travelling in the form of the soul?

Then it struck me! That was the key—imagination!

I focused all my energies into imagining myself on the other side of the wall and even as I was concentrating, I was on the other side!

Now all was clear and I was at the foyer, feeling bright like the sunshine that was coming through the windows.

Physical senses continue to remain in the physical body even when the soul is out of the body, while the soul has its own subtle senses.

Whenever the soul is out of the body and its senses perceive something during astral travel, they send signals back to the physical senses in the physical body. Because of this, when the soul returns to the physical body, the senses in the physical body remember all that which the soul perceived during its astral travel.

I again focused my energies and willed myself to see everything around me at once.

All things linear changed, giving me a 360-degree view.

The physical realm meant nothing as I could sense it no more.

There was a sensation of floating through everything. All I could feel of my being was a warm aura.

***

The soul has a mind, whereas a physical body has a brain. I understood this difference between these two entities.

Most importantly the mind works only through a thought or imagination.

So, as a soul, one has to think or imagine what one would like to do. And immediately that happens.

As I moved around in the room I understood that I didn't actually have to move, I needed only to imagine.

Everything and every sound was alive around me. I could hear the distant mundane chatter clearly. I walked through furniture, the coffee table, the glass jar, and the water in it. In turns and all at once, I was the table, the glass jar, and the water in it.

I realized that as a soul I was much smaller than an atom itself. Inside the atom also there is empty space and that empty space seemed to me as vast as the sky outside.

There were other things I heard, of course, others' conversations for which I wasn't the intended audience. They were now occurring more frequently and becoming so common place that it didn't seem out of this world.

I could now know what was impossible before. This astral form was so powerful it could see everything, yet not be seen.

I wanted to go beyond the walls of my house. If my astral form had no limitations, why should I even consider boundaries such as physical walls.

It was time to visit some old friends, with whom I had lost touch.

As I sat down for meditation I had only the names and faces in my mind. I thought solely about them and the universe must have been conspiring to my benefit because, to my luck, my four friends were meeting for some work. Even though I have been in the astral form for a while, something occurred to me for the first time. The astral me did not have to step out and conduct the journey following a physical route, through walls and other objects.

In a flash, I had travelled in the astral form and was among my friends. I felt I was hovering around them. They had finished their work and were bidding each other goodbye.

Next day a thought came to me of meeting my old friend who was in London. It was still an hour before sunrise, all was calm and quiet just the way I liked it. I closed my eyes and went through the meditation again for astral travel.

I saw him. He seemed a little chubbier than the last time I had met him.

He was walking from his parked car back towards his house. He still had that funny style of walking, putting his feet straight out like he were marching. I would have recognized him even if I had seen him from behind. But here I was, bang at his doorway right in front of him, and he walked right past me, never sensing my presence. I felt his energy brush past me, the astral me.

I had finally succeeded in coming to a faraway place with my efforts combined with the blessing of the universe. Before I could realize that I was leaving the physical body so far behind, I had been transported here. It was as if the miles of land and oceans between us did not exist. I had put all my efforts into doing this but, when it happened, the truth seemed more unbelievable than science fiction.

Brushing my disbelief aside, I followed my friend into

his home. He sat down in a chair and I went and placed myself right in front of him. I was overflowing with the joy of seeing an old friend, that too in this manner. My happiness must have been contagious, because I saw a smile playing on my tired friend's face for no particular reason.

"You seem to be in a good mood today, some new client project at work?" asked his wife.

"Nothing of that sort, dear, nothing special, I don't know why, but I suddenly felt very elated when I came inside. Like I had found something after a long time," he said.

I was overcome with fondness for him and felt like hugging him and I did not stop myself. I focused on giving him the tightest of hugs.

"Aaaah," whispered my friend.

"What's the matter?" asked his wife.

"I felt as if one of my old friends hugged me," he said half-anxious, yet half- smiling.

"What is wrong with you today? You are acting weird," she said.

"I don't know. Can you see anything? I am feeling strange things."

"Tell me the truth, are you taking drugs?" his wife demanded, anxiously.

"Don't you know me? Do you think I'm a teenager to experiment with things like that?" my friend retorted.

"No, these things keep coming in the news and I got worried when you behaved strangely," she replied.

"Never mind, forget it," he said staring away from his wife at the space next to her, which was where I was. If sparks could laugh, I would say I was laughing out loud. And I was, just not in a way that anyone there would notice. I had got what I had come for; it was time for me to leave.

I left his house and country, but travelled to even further lands. To places where there were no lands even.

Like an expert potter who plays with clay to give it any shape he imagines, I played with the possibilities of the travels of the soul. Could I see if other souls also existed in space?

I focused my meditation on this desire to see other souls. After days of efforts in this direction I finally saw flashes of souls floating in space as sparks of lights. I persisted and with some more practice I could clearly see them whenever I travelled outside the body.

Then a desire arose to interact with some of these souls.

Why were they here? Were all of them on a journey like mine? Had some souls slipped out of body in accidents?

I had heard of several people recounting their out-of-body experiences when they had near-death experiences. Were they a misstep in cosmic calculations? I wanted to know. Who else could I ask but the souls themselves?

I came near a soul, focused my energies on connecting with it. But there was no response. Perhaps the soul was in deep sleep. I tried again with several other souls but couldn't get any response from anyone. Couldn't they see me? Was I breaking some rule of this dimension?

In a deeper self-enquiry and observation of the subtle reality, I later realized that all those souls were floating in space after their physical bodies had died and were waiting for the next body. While waiting for the next body, the souls remained in a dream and deep sleep state. They could not wake up because they had no physical body to wake up in.

I was awake because I had realized the entity of my soul while being in the physical body. This awareness of being the soul would continue even after the death of the physical body.

A soul, which has not realized its existence as a soul while being in a physical body, remains unaware of this fact after the death of the physical body and hence it remains in the sleep or dream mode in space. In the dream state it keeps dreaming about its past birth connections with people and situations. All the impressions that were created in its previous births get randomly projected as dreams without any connection between one dream and the other.

People who are left behind by the departed keep remembering the soul as per their relationship, but the departed soul gets disconnected from them as it has already taken millions of births earlier and it randomly keeps dreaming about all those births' impressions and hence loses track of which are immediate birth relationships and which earlier birth relationships.

All worldly relationships, such as that of father, mother, brother, spouse, child, etc., remain confined only to the physical body. Once the physical body dies, the relationship also dies. The soul gets freed from all the attachments of the relationships that existed when it was in a physical body.

The soul waits in space for a suitable body for the journey of its next birth to settle its karmic accounts with all those with whom it had attachments, aversions, love, hatred, enmity, or other forms of connections.

I learnt to observe and ponder without questioning. My discoveries were endless.

Once I observed a flurry of activity and saw some souls rushing in a direction. I followed one soul and found that it suddenly entered an egg and disappeared. One soul went through a house and went into the abdomen of a woman and vanished. I realized that this is how souls acquire various physical bodies of different species after their previous bodies die and they leave them.

I saw, I felt, and I learnt that the more I learnt the more I felt there is more to learn and more to explore.

Even with all that I now know, why does something beckon me from the beyond? What is the calling? I don't know.

NECTAR OF GYANA:

- As the soul is made of light, it defies the laws of physical matter and resides in space when it is not in a physical body.
- The soul is so small and tiny that the space in between two atoms itself appears to be as vast as the sky.

- The soul while being in the body through its ego of 'I' considers itself to be like a huge mountain, even though it's just a speck in creation. One who realizes this truth becomes humble and grounded.
- The relationship between two people is only between the physical bodies. Once the soul discards the physical body, the worldly relationships with the other physical bodies also get discarded.
- When we realize and achieve the state of the soul while being in the physical body itself, we develop a free will to take birth wherever we want to, in whichever family we want to, and decide our own course of future births.

The Downpour

The parched earth quenched its thirst with the first rain, their union bringing out the sweetest smell of nature.

Swamiji sat cross-legged on a chair, his back erect and his face radiating effervescence, a soft glow, as always. His saffron robes accentuated his tall frame. In the mid-morning summer heat, he seemed to be a bright radiant presence, a sun on earth. The air was heavy with anticipation.

Looking at me, Swamiji asked, "How is your astral travel experience?"

"It's great, Swamiji. It's fascinating and full of joy. So many secrets have been revealed to me during this astral travel journey." I leaned forward, eager to take my spiritual journey forward. "What next, Swamiji?"

Swamiji kept quiet. I waited, expecting to be praised for what I had accomplished, and eager to know what other such supernatural stunts and feats I could perform under Swamiji's guidance.

Finally Swamiji spoke. "What you accomplished through astral travel is just a physical feat and not a spiritual one. Astral travel has nothing to do with spiritual evolution and ultimate enlightenment."

Swamiji looked at me in the eye and continued, "Astral travel is the biggest impediment to your spiritual progress and ultimate enlightenment. Even though only yogis through yogic sadhana can achieve astral travel, it has nothing to do with spiritual progress. It cannot take you to enlightenment."

The words struck me like a thunderbolt. I had thought I was on a path like no other and had progressed a lot spiritually, but Swamiji was saying that what I had experienced was actually an impediment to my spiritual progress? How? Maybe I hadn't put forth my question properly.

"Astral travel, Swamiji. The one that helps us overcome the fear of death? The one where we get out of the body while we are alive? This supernatural act is an impediment? How, Swamiji?"

Swamiji replied, "You have answered your question yourself. Tell me, what fears are you overcoming?"

"The first and biggest fear is the fear of death that one has to overcome," I said

Swamiji questioned, "Why worry about death? Everything that is born must die."

"But by crossing the threshold we can drive away the fear of perishing. We can move forward after discarding this fear of death," I said.

"Death is a reality that everyone has to face someday, and you shouldn't fear reality. If you are resisting the idea of perishing, you are still holding on to the idea of 'you'. That is the impediment in not knowing the goalpost. And if you are taking a detour from the path, there are chances that you may forget the path," Swamiji explained, calmly.

I felt lost. How could astral travel be an impediment? How could it make me lose the way? Hadn't I given up everything to reach the ultimate on this path? Was this not an important aspect of spiritual evolution? My mind buzzed with these thoughts.

"Swamiji, my understanding is limited. Please help me understand," I said.

"All the shaktis and siddhis, the supernatural powers, are impediments to spiritual progress as they have the tendency to boost ego and to be misused," Swamiji began. "Astral travel is just another physical progress and not spiritual progress. The traveller has access to subtle forms of the body, but it is still in the realm of physicality."

The atmosphere had turned intense. Whether I understood or not, I paid attention. Not many had seen Swamiji speak this way before. I clung to his every word.

"Spiritual progress is the expansion of consciousness. But here with astral travel, we are only trying to compete with birds or mechanical planes and rockets. Eagles while flying in the sky can see a piece of mutton miles away. This ability is not supernatural for the eagle, it is necessary for its survival. To be able to spot its prey even from heights that not many other birds fly in.

"Owls can see in the dark, bats are blind yet can fly at a high speed with precision without hitting any object, these are tools that nature has given them to survive.

"These are some of the natural powers these creatures possess. But the same powers, if adapted by a human being, are considered supernatural. Whatever our action is, if it isn't our natural progression, if it isn't what nature wills, are we really going on the true path?

"Now machines can do many things that were impossible earlier. But are these scientists who invented these machines considered spiritually evolved beings? Whether they use the tools in a laboratory or you use your own body, you are ultimately operating at the physical level.

"Humans try to compete with these creatures thinking that they are evolving spiritually. We are our own enemies sometimes, as doing something special can give people a feeling that they are equal to God. These practices create an additional problem of having to deal with the inflated ego. And thus, we are always running around in circles," Swamiji concluded.

This conversation left me dumbstruck. I was taken aback to learn that for all these years, the intense sadhana which I had been doing, under the guidance of Mamaji and now with Swamiji's blessings, to achieve astral travel was only a physical feat and not a spiritual journey. Still, everything was not clear to me.

Anything which an ordinary person cannot do but we can only boosts our ego. We start doing all that we are not supposed to do and start attracting public attention, being worshipped, being showered with money, name and fame and, in the process, lose track of our main goal of enlightenment. We again get entangled in the same maya which we were trying to escape.

Swamiji narrated a story from the Indian scriptures in which God says, "Millions worship me and want me. The first ring of maya that I throw around them is by fulfilling their worldly desires. Most of them stop wanting me but continue to worship me to safeguard what they have received from me.

"However, a small percentage of people continue to worship and want me. Around them, I throw the next ring of maya, by giving them name, fame, and a high position in the society. Again most of those people stop wanting me and get engrossed in the maya of money, name, fame, position, and status. Now it is they who start getting worshipped and the most obvious result of that is that they forget to worship me.

"A small handful of people resist this layer of maya too, and continue to worship me through various intense means of sadhana, yoga, meditation, etc. I bless these spiritual aspirants with supernatural powers, yogic shaktis, siddhis, etc., with which they attain a status almost akin to gods. In this state it would be next to impossible for them to continue their last leg of sadhana for enlightenment. They completely get immersed in their godly state. They stop performing any austerities and sadhana and justify their being satisfied with whatever they have achieved in the guise of uplifting other human beings.

"They do not realize that it's their ego of having achieved a feat which only a handful of humans can achieve in their lifetimes that makes them forget their main goal of seeking me, for which they started their spiritual journey in the first place. They do not realize that it's all a part of God's maya and they too get engrossed in that maya which has in some way or the other engulfed the whole world.

"Only one or two serious aspirants, who defy even these supernatural powers, shaktis, and siddhis, and do not consider them of any value in comparison to achieving and realizing God, eventually meet me and become one with me.

"These one or two divine souls, among the millions who started their journey to realize me but got entangled midway in my maya, are the lucky ones who realize me in my true aspect. They are the only ones to know who I am and who they are, what my nature is, how I exist, what I do, how I operate this universe and my true nature and their true nature of being formless, omnipresent, and in an omnipotent state."

I was dumbstruck. All the astral travel I had done seemed to fade into insignificance in comparison to what Swamiji had just explained about achieving God and ultimate enlightenment. I felt ashamed of wanting something which is part of the grand maya of God. I had all along been pursuing something which was of no significance in the overall scheme of things and had taken me no closer to the goal I actually wanted to pursue.

I fell at Swamiji's feet and asked for forgiveness. I told him I no longer want to pursue astral travel if it was just a physical achievement and not a spiritual one. I did not want to get caught in the cycle of maya again, having left it behind and come so far towards realizing the ultimate self.

Oh Swamiji, please take me towards my enlightenment, I prayed!

Swamiji smiled and continued his gyana.

"The universe seems simple and complex at the same time," he said. "In truth, it is neither. It simply exists. Our gaze, our mind, attributes meaning to everything."

Swamiji's voice rang clear. It had a unique quality of sound, a pure clarity that was yet soft with kindness. He continued to speak, explaining concepts and secrets beyond my comprehension. I did not even blink. My gaze was fixed on him.

Like a sponge, I was absorbing everything he spoke even without knowing what it was. I knew I was receiving something I had sought. What had I sought? And what was I receiving? I didn't understand and I couldn't explain if asked. But it felt like a thirst of many lifetimes was getting quenched. My mind was like a fully open sunflower, receiving sunlight. Like nature, existing simply in the reality of the moment.

Cosmos, vibrations, universal forces, static and dynamic consciousness, self, atman, brahmanda, super consciousnes, Shiva shakti—Swamiji spoke of all this and more, and I listened, more with my heart than my ears.

To understand the enlightened, I needed to tune in

with bhava. I visually filled my mind by simply staring at Swamiji, and between us, time itself stood suspended.

An energy circle had formed around Swamiji. An all-encompassing circle that made me forget my own existence, my physical body and every pleasure and pain attached to it. The spiritual music in me reached a crescendo, a peak.

And out of nowhere, the bright sunny day turned dark. Black stormy clouds moved rapidly and engulfed the sky. A flash of lightning, a loud clap of thunder, and then came the downpour, like the heavens were emptying every drop they had. It rained and rained, till there was nothing else in the moment but rain.

Swamiji stopped speaking. He retreated into a deep silence. I too sat in silence.

Nature spoke through the cloudburst of rain. I was suspended in an indescribable, unimaginable state. Finally the rain stopped, slowly subsiding to a drizzle and dripping from leaves.

The rain had washed everything and renewed it. All that was there before seemed like a new entrant on the scene—the trees, the birds, and a faint noise of water dripping on a tin roof in a distance.

"It is a celebration by nature," Swamiji smiled as he spoke. *"Whenever a saint connects with the oneness of the universal divinity with the intense flow of gyana and bhava, nature graces the moment with some form of physical manifestation to assure us of the experience."*

I looked outside and again at Swamiji, feeling that I had been blessed even before I had asked for it.

It was just pure bliss. An experience that would define my life to come.

"Where is my food? I am hungry," said Swamiji.

And like one who has snapped out of hypnotism, I also felt hungry all at once. During the past four hours, I had not even realized the existence of my body, and now the stomach was making its presence felt, bringing me down to the earth.

Slowly, Swamiji stood up. I showed my gratitude by prostrating before him. As he rose, I had in my mind a question and looked at Swamiji, wondering if this would be the right time to ask.

"Swamiji, today you have revealed so much, so many layers of revelations, secrets of universes, the creator and its creation, self and the Supreme Divine Being. I feel like there is something which got absorbed in me but I do not know what it is. I felt so mesmerized and connected with you and the subject that I do not remember anything that you said and I fear all your effort must have gone waste," I said.

"In the soil of your soul, the seed has been sown. Wait till you see the seed sprout and grow into a big tree laden with nectar-filled fruits to understand what I have said," said Swamiji patting my back and walking way.

Irrespective of whether we understand or not, a gyani's gyana never goes waste. It is given to us with the power of his enlightened state and the power to understand at the right time, in the right place, and with the right perspective. All one has to do is listen to a gyani in his proximity and everything else is taken care of by his grace.

The experience of the afternoon began to brim and boil over in my heart. I had spent such a long time in yogic sadhana, experienced the very limits of pain and endurance, and I had experienced what many could not even fathom, like astral travel. I had lived in austerity and detachment yet, no physical, intellectual, or even what I thought were spiritual experiences, could match this experience that Swamiji had bestowed upon me.

I hadn't understood the words themselves that Swamiji had spoken; yet they had moved me and shaken me to my core. How had I been so transfixed and felt oneness with the universe, even though I hadn't tried it consciously or through meditation?

I understood the limitations of intellect, physical, and yogic sadhana too. I began to grasp the ultimate power of consciousness.

I had been drawn to Swamiji from the moment I had seen him. If there ever was any hesitation, it was wiped away today.

During my time with Swamiji, I had gone through a range of emotions: of awe, of service, of being tested as a disciple. This moment, this afternoon, had sealed the relationship.

It was . . . a complete surrender.

NECTAR OF GYANA:

- Pure spirituality does not recognize astral travel as significant to spiritual progress. Even though it is fascinating, it can be the cause for downfall in one's spiritual path.
- We should worship God not with worldly desires but only to realize him. Once we realize God, then automatically everything in the world will be taken care of. But if we seek worldly desires, then realizing God will not be taken care of.
- Enlightenment is about knowing and realizing our entity as the pure consciousness, and it is not about projecting shaktis, siddhis, or name and fame to attract crowd.
- Surrendering ourselves at the feet of a spiritual guru is the biggest and the most difficult sadhana, and that alone can take us to an enlightened state.
- Nothing significant can be achieved in the spiritual path without the grace of a guru.

Guru—The Source of Light

As per the Indian tradition, a guru—the spiritual master—has great significance, as he is the one who makes the spiritual aspirant realize his true self and realize God. Guru is regarded even higher than God, as without him no one can realize the true state of God and the truth about the universe.

Even Kabirdasji said:

'Guru Gobind dono khade, kake lagon paay
Balihari Guru aapno, Govind diyo bataay.'

When the Guru and God are standing together, one should first bow down to the Guru as it is only because of him that God has descended before the aspirant.

Guru has several meanings in Sanskrit.

(1) 'Gu' means 'Darkness' and 'Ru' means 'Remover'. Guru is one who removes the darkness of ignorance and ignites the light of knowledge.

(2) 'Gu' also means 'Gunatheeta', or 'beyond attributes', and 'Ru' means 'Rupavarjita', or 'beyond form'. One who is himself beyond attributes, who does not attribute any action to himself and is established beyond the limitations of form is a guru.

(3) 'Gu' means 'Maya', Illusion, and 'Ru' means 'Supreme Divine Knowledge'. One who is capable of removing the illusions of this world and bestows pure divine knowledge upon us is a guru.

It is the guru and guru alone who can help an aspirant to cross over the worldly ocean and help in breaking the cycle of birth, death, and rebirth by enlightening the aspirant through pure divine knowledge and self realization.

Without a proper and enlightened guru it is almost next to impossible to transcend the illusory effects of the world and get liberated.

A guru is one who has left all worldly attractions and desires and has walked on the path of spirituality. He is the one who has experienced himself, through his spiritual sadhana, the oneness with the Supreme Divine Being and the omnipresent consciousness.

He is always established in the pure consciousness, and uses his physical body and mind for the upliftment of spiritual aspirants. He has no selfish desires of his own; his one selfless desire is to make spiritual aspirants realize their true self and to liberate them from the clutches of worldly maya.

A guru establishes his disciples in eternal bliss, who were otherwise caught in the cycle of happiness and sadness, joy and sorrow, pleasure and pain, success and failure. He rescues his disciples from these peaks of emotions, and helps them reach a state of equilibrium.

A guru is like a satellite that sees everything from high up in the sky, with a 360-degree vision and ability to perceive things in their totality. He knows the destination, the path which will take his disciple to the destination, the impediments and the obstructions in the path, and the support and the protection that the disciple requires from time to time.

There is a story in which one night a disciple saw a dream where he was walking along a beach. In this dream, when flashes of joyful situations and favourable circumstances of his life were seen, he saw four footprints on the beach, and when the flashes of adversities in his life were seen, he only saw two footprints.

He understood that the additional two footprints belonged to his guru, but he was surprised that during adversity, they seemed to desert him.

The next morning, he went to his guru and, having shared his dream with the guru, asked him in disappointment why he had left him alone during adversities.

With a smile the guru said, "My son, the two footprints

that you saw during your life's adversities were mine, not yours. Those were the times I carried you in my arms and walked the path for you."

Thus, a true guru not only guides his disciple along the spiritual path, but walks alongside the disciple himself and, during times of difficulty, lifts the disciple and carries him in his arms.

There are people who consider someone a guru only when they experience or witness some supernatural feats. They think that the very act of going to a guru should automatically resolve their problems. Even without any interaction, the guru should know what is going on in the mind of the aspirant, and be able to see the past, present, and future of all the people who visit him. People also feel that a guru should offer solutions to their problems and not merely give gyana or knowledge.

Most people go to a guru with a lot of worldly expectations, and only with the fulfilment of their expectations do they consider the person a guru. Neither are such people spiritual aspirants themselves, nor are the gurus who guarantee the solutions of worldly problems and fulfilment of worldly desires truly spiritual.

The guru should not be considered as a money-vending machine nor should the guru himself be a money-making machine. Gyana is not a product on sale and cannot be bought by paying money. Both are forbidden.

Surrendering to the guru and being in the proximity of the guru doesn't necessarily mean that the problems in life will cease to exist. Gurus such as Ramakrishna

Paramahansa, Ramana Maharshi, Shankaracharya, and, for that matter, all the avatars of God such as Rama and Krishna themselves had many problems in their lives.

Our karmas remain associated with us even after we find a guru. But being in the proximity of a guru, we won't feel the pain of the adversities and unfavourable situations.

All the pains and the feelings of sorrow that we go through are caused by ignorance. Once the veil of ignorance is lifted through the guru's gyana, even in adversities, we do not feel the pain. We just witness the adversity and allow it to pass. Through the gyana we become aware that just as favourable situations are temporary, so are unfavourable situations. They too are temporary and they come in our lives only to manifest the results of our past karma and then go away.

Instead of searching for a guru with miraculous powers, we should search for a guru with pure gyana. Miraculous powers may temporarily solve some of our life's problems but not permanently. Only pure gyana can solve life's pains and sorrows permanently.

The problems in life, and the pains and sorrows we feel, are the result of the darkness of ignorance and as a guru is the provider of the light of knowledge, these pains and sorrows vanish from life instantly when the gyana dawns in us. This is akin to how the darkness over thousands of years in a cave vanishes with the lighting of a single matchstick.

The broad parameters that can be used to gauge the

suitability of a guru and his spiritual prowess are that when we are in the proximity of the guru we feel at complete peace within our inner self, tranquil and meditative. Our mind remains locked without any thoughts and feels shameful in asking for solving trivial worldly problems or worldly desire fulfilment. A feeling of complete satisfaction, contentment, and fullness dawns upon us.

The attraction towards a guru gets created in such a way that we crave to be in his proximity as much as possible. A guru has the potential to transform an ordinary human being into an extraordinary being and bring our state equal to his own state.

Such is the magic of a guru!

Chandragupta Maurya was a poor, ordinary shepherd before he became the great Indian emperor. One day when he was practising archery, his arrows were hitting the tree but not the target.

Seeing this, Chanakya came to him and said, "Your technique is good but know that you should stop your breath when you release the arrow. The arrow should be drawn up to your ear before it is released."

Chandragupta did as Chanakya directed and he hit the target bang on. Chandragupta asked Chanakya, "Who are you? You do not seem to be a king."

Chanakya replied, "Though I am not a king, I can make someone a king. I have that potential." And he asked Chandragupta, "Do you want to be a king?"

"Yes. What do I have to do to become one?"

"You have to do nothing other than to blindly follow

me without any ifs and buts, reservations, conditions, restrictions, and excuses. You have to follow me and do what I ask you to do."

Chandragupta surrendered to him and went on to become the founder of one of the biggest empires across the Indian sub-continent. Such is the outcome of the meeting of a capable guru and a capable disciple.

Adi Shankaracharya equated guru with the 'bhringi keeda', the black bee. The black bee has no gender but still its population continues to grow. The secret is that the black bee picks up a new-born insect of other species and puts them in a hole of a tree or a wall.

The black bee, with its wings, constantly makes a 'brrr ... brrr' drone. Constantly listening to this sound, the new-born insect feels that the sound is coming from its body and slowly its body transforms into a physical body similar to that of the black bee which is capable of making the same 'brrr . . . brrr' sound.

Similarly, through continuous listening to the guru's spiritual gyana in his physical proximity, the disciple eventually achieves the state of the guru himself.

The objective of the black bee and guru are the same—to make others like them. Just as the other species of insects do not have to put in any effort into becoming the black bee, so is the case with an ordinary human being. We have to do nothing to get enlightened except surrender ourselves at the feet of an enlightened master. We only have to be like the insect, which hears nothing other than the sound of the black bee. We should also not listen to any other sound or gyana except that of our guru so as to become like a guru ourselves.

There is a famous couplet in Hindi:

'Paras mein aur guru mein bahu antaro jaan,
Woh loha kanchan kare, yeh kare aap samaan.'

Paras, the touchstone, can only convert iron into gold but cannot make the metal a touchstone like itself. But, a guru can transform the disciple to become like himself.

Think of the guru as a washer-man who washes away our sins, negativity from our minds, and the sanchit karmas we have accumulated, so as to give us salvation.

The guru can also be thought of as a beautician. We go to a beauty parlour to beautify ourselves whenever we feel our hair needs a cut or a trim, or the dead skin needs a peel, or the face needs cleansing, or stressed muscles need a massage. Similarly for inner beauty we should go to a guru to get unwanted layers of negative impressions peeled off, to shed an excess of ego, arrogance, and false pride, to massage the tired, depressed, rigid mind, to remove the clots of vengeance and revenge from the heart, to cleanse the soul and to clean our inner self from the filth of hatred, fear, and jealousy.

The guru, like the perfect beautician, helps project our true divine self, the atman, to ourselves.

The divine, peaceful, and blissful atman, which was buried under layers of worldly delusion, greed, aversions, and attractions, is gifted back to us in its original form by the guru. He knows which areas of our inner self need to be cleaned to reveal our own self to us.

What is required from our side is a regular visit to him and complete surrender; the rest will be taken care of by him.

Whenever we walk on the path of spirituality by surrendering ourselves at the feet of a guru, all our worldly matters, resources, conveniences, and spiritual plans are taken care of by the guru. Without the guidance, support, and grace of a guru we cannot tread on this path and achieve the ultimate.

Our problem most of the times is that we try to judge the guru rather than seek knowledge and blessings from him. When we try to judge someone, we judge them based on our limited knowledge, notions, and perceptions. This only means that we are searching for someone who is like us and similar to what we know.

How can we judge anyone who is more evolved than us, who is more knowledgeable than us, who is more experienced than us, whose revelations are unknown and unheard of, and who has become one with the universal infinite expansion?

When someone wants to give us more than what we know but in a different format, our mind doesn't accept it. Our mind accepts only that which is given in a way we want and not in a way which the guru wants to give.

A disciple went to his guru and asked him as to when he would get enlightened. The guru replied, "When you stop seeing."

The disciple asked, "What should I stop seeing?"

The guru replied, "When you stop seeing the unreal flowers and the unreal moon."

Confused, the disciple asked, "But when do I look at the unreal flowers and the unreal moon?"

The guru replied, "You yourself live an unreal life and when you stop living an unreal life, you will start seeing the real flowers and the real moon and then your life will also become a real life. We live in the world of words, and words are unreal. Words cannot convey the reality behind situations, people, emotions, and behaviour. There is always a hidden and underlying reality which remains unseen and unspoken. The explanations that we get for the worldly things are actually not like that in reality. So, we have to get liberated from words so as to get liberated from the unreal."

The disciple said, "Whenever I come to you I get confused."

The guru smiled and said, "Frankly, it is my job is to confuse you because unless you get confused, you will also not seek clarity."

People quickly jump to conclusions for everything that they see and experience in the world based on their perceptions, and that is what binds them to the world and creates a layer of ignorance.

Listening to a guru is an art. Whenever a person listens to a guru, he listens based on what he wants to hear, what impresses him, and what satisfies his conditions and not based on what the guru is trying to tell. In the process we miss out on many important things that the guru is trying to convey.

So if you want to get enlightened, go to a guru and listen to what the guru says and the way in which the guru says, and perceive with the same perception with which the guru wants you to perceive. You must learn to go with the flow of the guru's gyana and match his frequency without creating blockades in your mind and without filtering his gyana.

However, this is possible only when we unconditionally and totally surrender to a guru.

We are lucky if we get a guru in this lifetime, we are luckier if we are able to surrender at the feet of guru and we are the luckiest if the guru bestows his mercy on us. However we are unlucky if we cannot find the right guru, we are unluckier if we come across a guru but cannot recognize him, and we are the unluckiest if we find a guru and recognize him too but cannot surrender at his feet.

NECTAR OF GYANA:

- The word 'guru' itself is so soothing and is like music to our ears, as our soul has been seeking this precious being from the day it was separated from its source, the pure consciousness.
- Consciously or unconsciously somewhere the soul knows that it is the guru only who can reunite it with its source.
- The soul wanders in the world only in ignorance and

when the knowledge of its true self is imparted by the guru, it stops wandering and starts living joyfully.

- Surrendering at the feet of a guru means surrendering our existence itself as unless we surrender our false existence the guru will not be able to show us our real divine existence, just as only when the cloud drifts away, can we see the sun.

- Do not ask a guru, "Who are you? From where have you come?" Instead, when you go to a guru, ask him, "Who am I? From where have I come? What is the purpose of my life? Where am I going to go? What is my ultimate destination?"

Corpse of Life and Dance of Death

There are only two eternal realities in this world and nobody, not even God, can change these realities. These two realities are LIFE and DEATH.

Whoever is born in this world is going to die irrespective of whether one is rich or poor, a human or an animal. Even when the gods manifest in this world in a physical form, they leave the world by leaving behind their mortal body.

Every moment every soul in this world is moving towards this eternal truth of Death. Even if someone is born under very favourable planetary positions and living in a perfect Vastu/Feng-shui-compliant house, or born with good fate, or has performed good deeds in his past lives, still nobody can save him from the clutches of death. The fact is that we all are waiting for death and while waiting for this event called 'death' to take place, we are passing time in some way or the other.

Everybody's way of passing this time is different. Some pass the time making money, others by earning fame, or by managing family, state or country, or by running behind the attractions of life, or pursuing studies or giving discourses and performing religious rituals or spiritual practices. Every activity is only a pastime for the soul.

The difference in this 'pastime' between one person and another is only that some have passed their time happily and joyfully, while others have passed it in pain and sorrow. How we pass our time depends solely on us.

Imagine a big airport where thousands of passengers are waiting for their flights. While they wait, they all pass the time in different ways. Some gossip, others eat food, or shop, or play video games, or take naps or stroll around. Some are anxious, some are relaxed, some are stressed and some happily waiting for the departure time. Everybody's flight has taken off from some place to come to this airport and carry them to their destination. Similarly, our final flight, Death, has also taken off and is in the process of arriving in our life at some point or the other to take us to our ultimate destination.

Our life can also be compared to a train journey. The train is continuously on the move. We as passengers board the train at some station, and join the existing passengers who were travelling from earlier stations. We travel with them for some distance till a few of these passengers get down at some station and then some new passengers join us at that or another station. Similarly, we also get down at some station while the remaining passengers continue with their journey. This process of boarding and disembarking continues with various passengers.

This situation is the same in our lives—taking birth in a family and joining the existing family members is like boarding a train at some station and joining other passengers who are already in the midst of their journey.

Like co-passengers in the train, family members too can be of different natures, ages, and attitudes. Some are good, friendly, and affectionate, while others are uncaring and some others are rude and arrogant. However, having boarded the train, we have no other option but to travel and adjust with existing passengers. Similarly in real life, we should also adjust with our family members.

Just as a co-passenger may disembark at some station on the way, a family member too can die and leave us behind to continue with our life's journey. The co-passenger who had disembarked will catch another train going towards another direction; similarly, the family member who has died will take rebirth to join another family to continue his life journey in a new direction.

In the train journey, we do not develop any lasting attachment or enmity towards co-passengers even though we like some and do not like others, because we know that our journey with them is temporary and will come to an end sooner or later. But in real life, even though we know that our life journey too is temporary, since birth and death are inevitable, we still develop undue attachment with those who are good and friendly with us and develop aversion, enmity, hatred towards others who are not good to us. This attachment and aversion are a major cause for pains and pleasures in our life.

If there could be constant awareness about the life journey being akin to a train journey, with the joining and separation of co-passengers as an integral part of this journey, we will not develop undue attachment or aversion to anybody irrespective of their being good or otherwise. Our life journey will not have any peaks and troughs of high and low emotions. The sense of duty and responsibility will prevail over expectations and disappointments. Patience, tolerance, and forgiveness will become an indispensable part of one's attitude. Negative reactions will cease, as the subconscious impression of everything being temporary will be at the centre stage of our behaviour and attitude.

It depends on us what kind of a life we want to live while passing time and waiting for death and what kind of life we want to live after death, the life of a soul or the life of pure consciousness.

***

We were born millions of years ago as souls and since then have taken birth in physical bodies of millions of different species, including the human species. Every time we take birth in a physical body, it is to be understood as a transmigration stage, because after death we get into another physical body which can even be that of any other species. This means that there is no permanency in any body and we cannot be guaranteed a human body all the time.

This also implies that we must have no ego whatsoever of being born as a human being. It is only temporarily that we are in this body and nobody knows what we will be reborn as in our next life. We could be reborn as a human or as a dog, or snake, or a mosquito, bacteria, or even as a fatal cancer cell in somebody's body who may have been our own relative in some past birth.

The false pride of being wealthy, healthy, intelligent, and having a high status, position, and knowledge is temporary and that too is in a transmigration stage. Before we acquired these things, they had belonged to somebody else and after we have gone, they will belong to some others. We possess these things only temporarily but we develop a permanent ego.

The rule is that temporary things will give temporary happiness and permanent things will give permanent happiness.

As our body itself is temporary, everything which is related, connected, and acquired by the body is temporary too. We will leave all the things including the body behind, while carrying on with our journey beyond death.

Our next birth gets decided based on the intense and predominant last thought at the time of death. And our last thought generally is about that which we are excessively attached to, or feel enmity against, or fear the most.

Most people, during their lifetime, desire to remember

God at the time of their death but they remain ignorant of the fact that they cannot do so unless they have remembered Him all along their life with fairly good intensity and faith. When childhood is spent in ignorance, youth and middle age in lust, then how can one remember God during old age and at the time of death?

More importantly, since no one knows when death is going to strike, waiting for old age to remember God is foolish.

Lord Krishna has said in the Bhagvat Gita that 'the last thought of a person would be based on his attitude and behaviour during his lifetime'. If one has lived a life fully engrossed in the world with all kinds of emotions attached to it such as pains and pleasures, hatred, jealousy, and revenge, then his last thought will also be the same. He will not be able to remember God at the end.

Once, two disciples came to Lord Buddha and one of them while complaining about the other person, asked, "Lord, don't you think this man will be born as a dog in his next birth?"

When Lord Buddha asked why he thought so, the disciple replied, "This man is extremely attached to his dog. He goes for a walk with his dog, sleeps with his dog, and plays with his dog."

The Lord said, "This man may or may not be born as a dog but you will surely be born as a dog in your next birth, as more than him, it is you who thinks of his dog."

Just like a camera captures an image at the time of the click, certain images get clicked in the mind of the soul at the time of death based on one's attachments and aversions during life. These very images are caught hold of by the soul, which comes out of the body along with the life force. A suitable physical body which can take the soul to those places and among people matching these images attracts that life force and the soul then takes a rebirth.

If one is in the remembrance of God at all times, even while performing ones worldly duties without any fear or attachment, then at whatever time death strikes, there is no worry because he will leave the body peacefully and merge with the Supreme Divine Being. In addition, remembering God at all times helps one remain relaxed and connected to the higher consciousness, thus attracting good things and happiness in life while one is still alive.

Therefore, remaining established in the remembrance of God at all times is a profitable proposition, not only from a spiritual point of view but even from worldly point of view.

God can be remembered through any name or form as Rama, Krishna, Jesus, Shiva, Durga or through the formless divine energy, atman, brahmanda or pure consciousness.

NECTAR OF GYANA:

- Death is a temporary event, life is eternal. There is life after death and we can choose the kind of life we want after death.
- Our predominant nature during our lifetime and our

thoughts and feelings at the time of death decide the type of our next birth.

- We must learn to live a life without any attachment or aversion to anything or any person. Such life will not only be joyful throughout the life journey, but will become the door for ultimate salvation.

Purpose of Human Life

At some point of time in everyone's life, the question arises as to what the purpose of human life is? Why are we born and what is the purpose of our lives?

In the absence of any clarity, most people live life for the sake of living. Living life without any direction is like wandering in a jungle not knowing whether we are going deeper into the jungle or getting out of it.

There is a Hindi couplet which means: 'Run till you can run as you are only running seeing others running, but you will get what you want only when you stop running and come out of ignorance'.

In the race to become wealthier, more famous, better than others, are we not missing something in life? Peace, a good night's sleep, harmony in relationships, health, culture, character, concern, love and compassion: is there any place in our busy lives for these things?

In the worldly race, we forget what exactly the motive is behind all the running. Is it just to win against others in a competition or to gain something which we don't have or to show to others that we are also competent to run the race of life?

But the fact is that we lose a lot in this race, which we already possess, but remain unaware of. Peace, happiness, love, care, and compassion are all our inner possessions which is our God-gifted wealth, but we lose this most precious of wealth in our pursuit of material wealth.

Human birth is certainly not without a purpose. We are the most special species of all the 84 lakh known species in the universe with an enormous potential for intellect, wisdom, growth, free will, revelations, construction, destruction, recreation and emotions.

The purpose of human life is five-fold:

1. To be progressive: As the creator Himself is progressive, we are also expected to be progressive. We have been sent here by the creator to evolve materialistically, intellectually, emotionally, and spiritually. Through a progressive attitude, we tune into the frequency of the creator. However, our ego of doer-ship blocks this tuning. We get so caught up in the chaos of evolving materialistically that we end up forgetting that we are expected to evolve spiritually as well. We attribute our

success to ourselves and take pride in it whereas He expects us to attribute all our achievements, success, growth and possessions to Him.

2. To enjoy His creation and live happily: He has given everything to everyone in order to enjoy life, based on what each one deserves and what can give happiness to him, yet we complain about insufficiency because of our expectations and comparisons with others and feel unhappy. We have surrendered our happiness to our expectations, ego and comparisons. We should enjoy His creation as it is as we have whatever it takes to be happy.

3. To spread happiness: Not only should we always remain happy, but we should also spread happiness around us. He wants us to follow His concept of seeking happiness in others' happiness as He Himself has created this universe for the happiness of others and not for Himself.

   Poornananda Swamiji often used to say, *"The joy of seeing other's joy is a greater joy than our own joy."*

4. To liberate ourselves from the worldly entanglement and go back to our source: Even though we have been sent here for a temporary period and with some specific objective, we have forgotten that fact and have got engrossed in the attractions of the world. He wants us to come back to Him and remain in eternal bliss.

5. To help others get liberated: It is important to understand that our purpose does not stop at

enlightening ourselves. We have to persistently try to help others around us get liberated as well.

NECTAR OF GYANA:

- Life is not purposeless but unfortunately we limit our lives to worldly purposes. The world is temporary and worldly objects and people too are temporary, but life is eternal. Hence, the purpose of life has to be to seek eternity.

- We must learn to live life joyfully ourselves as well as spread joy all around us. These become the parallel purposes of life within the totality of seeking eternity.

- Growth and progress is inevitable in the universe. The universe is progressing constantly but if we do not keep up with its growth and progress, then we will be cast down the evolutionary ladder from the human species to a lesser-evolved species.

- Out of the 8.4 million known species, human species is the most special one as the human attributes are not found in any of the other species. So having been born as humans, we must realize how blessed we are and we must seek a purpose higher than the human birth itself.

Desire to be Desireless

J ust as the wind is the cause for waves in the ocean, desire is the cause for disturbance in the mind.

A desire-less mind is peaceful, calm, and relaxed. Desires, including unfulfilled desires, disturb this calmness. Unfulfilled desires irritate and frustrate the mind and fulfilled desires generate new desires leading to expectations, anxiety and worries. Out of new desires, only a few get fulfilled and others remain unfulfilled and we get caught in this vicious cycle of expectations, frustration, and disappointments.

However, everyone needs certain basic amenities in life such as a house to live in, money to buy food and clothing, perhaps a personal vehicle, a bit of entertainment, and savings to take care of future exigencies. But the confusion is how to differentiate between desire and necessity and strike a balance between the two.

Necessity is born out of compulsion to live, whereas desire is born out of competition. Desire springs from the ever active, unsatisfied senses and mental comparisons with what others have that we don't.

Desire is never constant but ever increasing. A deer in a hot desert sees what appears like water in the distance and runs towards it. On reaching the spot, though, it finds nothing. Instead the mirage appears further away in the distance. Pursuing desires is akin to the deer pursuing an illusory desert mirage.

There once lived a rich man in a villa. Opposite to his villa, lived a poor man in a hut. The rich man's wife used to observe the peace with which the poor man and his wife lived. It was a peace she herself never felt, neither in herself nor in her husband. Once when her guru visited her house, she sought to know why was it that even though they eat rich and healthy food they still fall sick whereas the poor couple hardly eat anything yet remain healthy. Why was it that they found it difficult to sleep even in air-conditioned bedrooms, but the poor couple slept like a log even in their uncomfortable hut. Why was it that they always lived in fear of the unknown even though their future was well secured, but the poor couple seemed fearless despite their precarious future.

To answer the question, the guru asked the rich lady to put some gold coins in a bag and told her to leave the bag in the poor man's hut in the night. Next day, as he was leaving, he told the rich lady to observe the poor man's family for next few months.

A couple of days later, the rich lady noticed that the poor man, who used to come back home early every evening, had started returning late in the night. Occasionally, she began to hear quarrels between the poor man and his wife. She observed the poor man's failing health and the wrinkles of tension on his face.

The rich man's wife was bemused at these developments. She had thought that after getting gold coins the poor couple will look even more happier and healthier than before but the opposite had happened.

Upon enquiry she came to know that the poor man, after finding the couple of gold coins in his house, desired to add more to them so as to secure his future, buy a house and other luxuries. He started working double shift, cutting down on his food and started consuming alcoholic drinks to overcome his stress. He also forced his wife to work and earn so as to save more money.

This changed attitude caused a lot of stress to the poor couple. They had no time for each other. They forgot what they had and started bothering about what others had that they didn't.

They forgot to live in the present and started living in the future thus losing their comfort zone of love, contentment, compassion and gratitude towards God, and getting entangled in illusory competition and eventually losing their peace.

And this is why it is often said by saints and scriptures

that desire is the main cause of mental disturbance. Even Buddha said, "Desire is the root cause of all evil."

There are desires that give pain and bind us to the world and there are desires that give us joy and liberate us. Three types of desires give pain, sorrow and disappointment and three types of desires give joy, happiness and salvation.

Desires which give pain and sorrow are:

1. Desire to acquire more and more things like wealth, name, fame, position, status, reputation, etc. The nature of these desires is such that even when they get fulfilled, they give birth to new desires and if those are not fulfilled, they cause tremendous disappointment. One is never satisfied with what one has and never reaches contentment, hence one is always in a state of discontentment, pain, sorrow, struggle, competition, and comparison.

2. Desire to be freed of pain, sorrows, adverse situations, bad luck and troubles and to be free of people who give pain and sorrows. It is a foregone conclusion that pain, sorrows, personal and professional losses will keep occurring in our life. So, the desire of a pain-less and a sorrow-less life will never get fulfilled, and this unfulfilment will cause further dejection and sorrow.

3. Desire to always get favorable results for all efforts, actions, reactions, activities, expectations, and karmas. Here, we forget that a life situation is not just the result of our present effort but is a combination of past karmas, past thinking and emotions, others negativity

and positivity (blessings and curses) towards us and our bahviour and attitude towards others. So, regardless of how strongly we desire a favorable result, there is no guarantee of achieving it.

As there is no rule in the universe that whatever we desire will get fulfilled, that too within our expected time frame and in the way we prefer, there is always a component of disappointment and sorrow in these desires.

Desires which give joy, peace, happiness, and salvation are:

1. Desire to be desire-less: This is when one is content with what one has and does not desire to acquire anything more. In fact, one is grateful to God for whatever he has given and uses the available resources to help others, uplift the downtrodden, serve the poor and aged, promote and protect nature, and pursue religious sentiments.

2. Desire for everybody's happiness, success, health, wealth, growth, prosperity, harmony: In this case, one does not want even one's enemies to suffer in any way and one is always in a mode of forgiving and seeking forgiveness. Prayers for everybody's wellbeing is the most important aspect of a life consumed by this desire: *'loka samasta, sukhino bhavantu'* meaning every soul in the universe may be happy, healthy and joyful.

3. Desire for salvation, liberation and enlightenment: This is the desire to get freed from the vicious clutches

of karma and from the cycle of birth, death and rebirth. The desire to attain enlightenment and moksha is considered to be the most ideal desire for a human being to have.

These three desires are godly desires and divine in nature hence are the givers of peace, happiness and eventual liberation. When we desire these things even God helps us fulfil these desires as they are of godly nature.

So, now the choice is ours regarding what to desire and what not to desire!

NECTAR OF GYANA:

- The universe has enough to satisfy our need but not our greed. Intense and unending desires convert into greed. We suffer not in the process of fulfilling our needs, but in the process of fulfilling our greed.
- The mind's nature is to remain calm and peaceful, but desires create disturbance in the mind.
- Desires are the result of comparisons, competition and expectations. Desire comes with an attachment of pain and suffering. Non-fulfilment gives pain, and fulfilment gives birth to new desire.
- Desire is usually related to worldly objects. The desire to become desireless, on the other hand, is not considered a desire. Worldly desires bind us and desirelessness liberates us.

Engineering Happiness

We are bestowed with natural happiness. That is our natural state and we don't have to do anything to be happy. But since we find it difficult to remain without doing anything, we become unhappy. To be happy, we have to stop doing all that which makes us unhappy. The behavioral aspects which take away our happiness need to be avoided, such as friction with others, conflicts, unnecessary arguments, expectations, desires and enmity.

Instead of discarding this negative nature from our mind, we seek happiness outside in the worldly objects or in the worldly people. They might give happiness temporarily but cannot give eternal happiness.

It is like using a deodorant to mask body odour, instead of keeping our body clean. The deodorant will have its effect only for some time and will then wear off, allowing the bad odor to emanate from the body again.

We are like sandalwood, whose nature is to emanate a fragrant smell. Sandalwood has to do nothing to emanate its fragrance, but if it is covered by layers of dust and filth then it will not be able to emanate its natural fragrance.

Similarly, we are naturally happy beings, but if we fill our minds with the layers of negative thoughts, jealousy, hatred and enmity, then our natural happiness does not get projected or experienced.

Even if the sandalwood is not covered with dust and filth, if we keep a piece of asafoetida next to it, the latter's smell is so strong that it doesn't allow us to smell the sandalwood fragrance. Likewise, if we are in the vicinity of negative people, who are prone to getting angry and irritated and having emotional outbursts, then too we will remain deprived of the inner happiness which is constantly available to us.

Happiness has two aspects—real and unreal. Unreal happiness is temporary and is found in worldly objects, but real happiness is eternal and found in the inner self. Real happiness can never be achieved if it is dependent on or associated with something unreal. This world is considered to be unreal and the atman is real.

Essentially, anything that undergoes change, or is impermanent and short-lived, can be considered unreal. Anything which has a limited lifespan and which is born or created, and which gets destroyed over a period of time is unreal.

There is nothing in the universe that does not change. There is nothing in this universe that is permanent and does not get destroyed. Everything is undergoing the process of change, whether it is physical matter or a physical body. Our body is constantly changing and is becoming older by the minute. It is heading towards death from the moment it is born. Similarly the thoughts of our mind change, our emotions change and so does everything else in our lives—money, wealth, house, car. In the larger world, the weather and even the mountains and oceans are constantly undergoing change.

Since everything is changing, everything could be construed as unreal. It is a different issue that everything is changing at its own pace. Everything has a lifespan, be it 1 minute, 1 hour, 1 day, 1 year, 100 years, 1000 years or 100000 years, and that which has a lifespan, is constantly moving towards the end of its lifespan. This is because everything in this creation is within the ambit of 'time and space'. Time and space are never constant, they are ever changing, and so is everything within them.

There is only one thing in this creation which does not change and that is atman, the divine self, the pure consciousness. There is never any change in the consciousness. It is static and eternal as it is beyond time and space. Since it never takes birth, it never dies and that which does not take birth and does not die, does not undergo any change also.

When we seek happiness in unreal objects such as wealth, house, jewelry, clothes, car, or in people like spouse, parents, children and friends who too are unreal and changing every moment, how can we get real happiness?

If we want real, everlasting and permanent happiness then we should seek it in the real, eternal and unchangeable atman, the self.

Whenever we get happiness in worldly objects or worldly people, it is in fact not happiness derived from them, but actually our own happiness which is hidden within our inner self that gets invoked through outer means.

If we realize this secret, then instead of searching for happiness in worldly objects and people, we can search for happiness within our own self and invoke that inner happiness without any medium whatsoever. Our inner happiness is our property, abundantly available within our inner self, and never gets depleted. The more we invoke our inner happiness, the more the inner self draws happiness from the universe and fills our hearts.

Thinking about the inner self, meditating and contemplating on it will help us get connected with it. Every thought, every emotion should be considered to have emanated from the self. Every object and every situation should also be considered to have emanated from this self, then even when the object changes, we will continue to enjoy permanent happiness as we would have attributed everything to the permanent self. This is the only way to attain permanent and long-lasting happiness in this world.

An old saintly lady was searching for something outside her hut when one of her disciples came to visit her. Seeing her searching for something, he also joined in. Seeing them both search for something, some more disciples who arrived on the scene, also started searching.

Unable to find anything even after searching for some time, one of the disciples finally asked the lady saint what she was searching for.

She said, "I am searching for the needle I lost."

Then the disciple asked exactly where she had lost the needle. The lady saint said she had lost it inside the hut. The disciples laughed. "Mataji, if you had lost the needle inside the hut then why are you searching for it outside?"

She replied with a smile, "Because there is no light in my hut and there is light outside. I am searching for my needle in the light."

"But Mataji, we have to search for the lost object wherever it was lost and not elsewhere just because there is light available there."

The saint replied, "This is what I have been telling you all along—to seek happiness in your inner self, but why is it that you all are searching for the same in the outer world?" She continued, "Just as I am searching for my needle outside the hut because there is some light available to see, you also search for happiness outside yourselves just because you see things outside you that are perceived by your senses as attractive. You have lost your happiness not in objects but in your inner self, and you too have to search for it only where you have lost it."

Even though human beings have been bestowed with a tremendous amount of potential and also with the availability of all those things in this world which can make them happy, yet it is found that most people are unhappy and unsuccessful.

There are broadly five qualities of unhappy people, because of which they are not able to lead a satisfactory life and enjoy happiness:

1. They are always complaining: These people are never happy with anything they have and with anything that is happening around them. They always complain about everything. If it rains, they complain about the rain and when the sun shines, they complain about the heat. When they fail in something, they complain about the non-cooperation of others and when they fall sick, they complain about bad food, or pollution, or contaminated water, or cloudy weather or some such thing.

2. They act before they think: These people act impulsively and regret their actions later on. They do not think about the pros and cons of their actions and, when they fail or face obstructions, they repent their decisions. The most common mistake people make is that they make commitments when they are too happy and take decisions when they are disturbed or angry, both of which have long-term implications that are not considered in the heat of the emotion. For example, in the momentary joy of someone's good performance a big commitment is made to gift him an expensive car and later repented when the same performance is not repeated. And sometimes, a heated argument

over some trivial matter leads people to break off a relationship altogether.

3. They talk more and listen less: These people have the habit of talking too much and not listening to others. They do not realize that when they talk, they talk based on what is already known to them but when they listen to others, they may learn something new. Since they do not listen to others, their growth comes to a standstill, and because of their habit of talking excessively, others keep a distance from them.

4. They dwell in the past: These people have a habit of living in the past. They remember the painful past incidents of their life and in this process they miss out on the enjoyment of the present. They perceive everything which is happening in their life based on past experiences, thus unconsciously creating more such painful situations in the present.

5. They give up easily: These people get disappointed and depressed easily. They have no resilience in the face of failures and they lose self-confidence at the drop of a hat. They have very little patience and are usually negative about their future. They do not realize that patience and perseverance is the key to success.

It is a well-known fact that no growth, be it personal, professional, or spiritual, can take place without a peaceful mindset. A peaceful mindset is directly related to our behaviour and attitude but, unfortunately, not many people bother to check and control that.

Now that these five qualities of unhappy people are known, all we have to do is consciously stay away from these habits and instead adopt the following five qualities to remain happy and peaceful:

1. Do not interfere in others' matters: It is a normal human tendency to interfere in others' matters and offer unsolicited advice. Irrespective of whether our advice is needed or not, and whether we are qualified to offer advice or not, we still go ahead and offer it. This is annoying to other people especially when they have not asked for it. What's worse, we don't stop at offering advice, but even try to monitor its implementation and in the process, embarrass people and force them to emanate negativity against us.

2. Do not crave for recognition: It is an inherent quality of humans to constantly crave recognition for all that they do. This creates an expectation from others and the nature of expectation is such that it never gets satisfactorily fulfilled so we end up feeling disappointed and dejected. There is a famous saying in Hindi— *'neki kar aur dariya main daal'*—which means to do good for others and then forget about it.

3. Do not be jealous of others: Most people are not happy with what they have, and crave instead for more and more. Their focus is always on what they don't have, rather than on what they do, so they tend to be jealous of others who appear to be better off.

The cause of jealousy could be anything, from physical looks, intellect, name, fame, to wealth, house, prosperity, or position. Jealousy keeps one forever unhappy and unsettled. We should consciously make an effort to not be jealous and instead be happy for what we have and what others have achieved. We must realize that God is not biased in giving somebody less and others more; everything depends on the individual's karma. We must accept everything that we have as a gift from God and know that He is the best judge to decide what and how much is good for each individual.

4. Grasp the best and leave the rest: All around us, we have good and bad people, good and bad things, and good and bad situations and it is up to us what we want to focus on. Generally our focus is only on the bad aspects of people, situations and things and hence we land up grasping only the bad. If we start grasping the good from all around us we will become happy and experience a growth in our personality. An oft-repeated example in spiritual literature is that of the lotus flower—the lotus flower blooms amidst all the dirt and muddy water around it. It is aware of all the dirt around it, but yet it just absorbs whatever it needs to absorb from the dirt for its own growth and blooms into a beautiful flower. Similarly, there might be all types of people and situations around us but it is entirely up to us to absorb the best from them for our own growth.

5. Do not make a habit of pointing out shortcomings of other people: We often tend to point out faults in those around us. Some people do it unintentionally and some do it intentionally with the motive of trying to correct those faults and change the other person for the better. But what people don't realize is that repeatedly pointing out flaws can act as a negative affirmation in the other person's mind and instead of changing for the better, the other person might feel dejected and depressed! Another outcome of repeated fault-finding could be that of strained relations and friction with the other person. The other person might get fed up of our fault-finding and would want to spend lesser and lesser time with us. Keeping these key points in mind, it is advisable to not indulge in repeated fault-finding in others.

It is only human beings out of all other 8.4 million species, who have the potential to be happy and peaceful as per their free will. Unfortunately, not many people use this potential and get swayed by favourable and unfavourable situations, good and bad people, right and wrong judgements and, as a result, get caught in the peaks and troughs of pains and pleasures, and happiness and sorrow.

Invoke your inner potential and use your free will to be happy all the time irrespective of situations and circumstances.

NECTAR OF GYANA:

- Happiness is in the inner self and not in the outside world. Happiness is not in objects or favourable situations; these are only the medium to invoke our own inner happiness. Know this secret and invoke inner happiness unconditionally.
- We should stop doing all that which makes us unhappy such as getting into arguments unnecessarily, creating friction and conflicts, and not accepting situations and people as they are. This will automatically keep us happy.
- The joy we take in others' joy should be a bigger joy than our own joy.
- None of us can get the best of everything in life but we should learn to make the best out of everything available to us and be eternally happy.

Unity in Variety

The whole of creation is one single united form of pure consciousness. This unity may not be visible and felt because of the limited perceivable capability of the mind and senses, but it is real. The unity among the seen and the unseen, physical and non-physical, form and formless is perfect and indivisible. Duality does not exist in creation. The universe is a highly homogeneous, non-dual creation of the consciousness.

Creation is nothing but a grosser manifestation of the subtlest, formless, pure consciousness. Pure consciousness is eternal and omnipresent. Even when creation did not exist, pure consciousness existed in its original, formless, subtle state. At the time of manifestation of creation, changes in the pure consciousness start taking place. It starts becoming grosser and grosser. The first identifiable stage of the grosser pure consciousness is ether which is the foremost and subtlest of the five elements. Further stages are air, fire, water, and earth. The combination of these five elements in various proportions causes the formation of all objects, including physical bodies.

Since pure consciousness converts itself into gross matter, everything can be said to be pure consciousness including the seen and unseen. There is nothing in creation that is not pure consciousness. Everything is homogeneously in unity with each other.

Normally, this unity remains hidden due to the limitations of the mind and limited perceptive capabilities of senses. However, knowledge of the ultimate truth of the lone existence of pure consciousness and regularly practicing meditation on this truth expands the horizon of the mind and breaks the perceptive limitations of the senses. It allows one to establish oneself in and perceive this unity in all creation.

One who sees unity in a variety of different objects and beings in creation, is evolved spiritually and is considered to be a seer of the real truth.

Perceiving the variety of creation as unconnected to one another and unconnected to its source is ignorance, maya. The delusion is created because the source, to which everything is connected, remains unseen and is beyond the perceptions of the senses. Whoever is able to overcome the ignorance and establish himself in the true knowledge transcends maya and escapes the cycle of birth, death, and rebirth.

Beings are nothing but the reflection of pure consciousness. Do not attribute the actions of various beings to pure consciousness as beings act based on the nature and qualities of their sense organs which they acquire during the grossification process of the universe. See the consciousness in all the beings and enjoy its oneness.

When you unite with the self, the consciousness, then you will see the same 'self' in others, behind the façade of their physical body, mind, and senses and also see others in yourself. In everything you will see the same self. This is perfect unity.

Pure consciousness itself having manifested from formless to form became many and, over a period of time, the many became too many, and the 'self' in the process of manifestation forgot that it is one that has become many and began to look at many as separate, and not the unified one.

You are not what you think you are and what you appear to others. Neither are you what you experience yourself to be. You are the 'self', the cause of the physical body and the provider of the power of consciousness. You are in perfect union with pure consciousness.

The variety in the world is an illusion. Even though the *whole universe is one single block of consciousness*, yet because of the different forms, shapes, and names given to different objects, they appear to be distinct and separate from each other. This is what is maya.

One of the best ways to understand this is to consider

the various forms of milk. When the milk is set, it is called 'curd' even though curd is nothing but the modified milk. When curd is churned, a separation takes place, which results in 'butter' and 'buttermilk'. Butter and buttermilk are not separate from the curd. Further, when the butter is heated up, it gets converted into 'ghee' (clarified butter). In each of these cases, it is only the change in form and nature of the original substance that results in a different substance that we recognize with a new name.

When the milk is split, we get 'cottage cheese' out of it. In this case also, even though it is nothing but milk, yet because of a new form and a new nature it has been given a new name as cottage cheese. When this cottage cheese is further processed, the product undergoes some more changes and develops some new qualities thereby giving it new names such as mozzarella, cheddar, and feta cheese.

All of these products—curd, butter, buttermilk, ghee, and cheese—are only a modified form of the milk, and they are not separate or distinct from it. Yet because of the modification, a new form came into existence and new names were given to each product, and they got perceived as different items from milk. This is called 'roop maya' and 'naam maya', the maya of form and the name.

Another example is of ocean water. Because of the heat of the sun the ocean water (visible) evaporates and becomes water vapour (invisible). This water vapour converts into cloud and again falls back as rain water. This rain water falls on earth and flows as river and merges back into its source, the ocean.

All of these things—water vapour, cloud, rain, and river—are only modified forms of ocean water and they are never separated from each other irrespective of whether they were visible as one block of water or not. This is another example of 'roop maya' and 'naam maya', the maya of form and the name.

Similar is the maya in the universe. Even though everything in the universe is the modified form of one single consciousness, because of the various forms and names given to various stages of modification and because of the same being in formless state at some point of time, we get deluded and start perceiving them as different and distinct objects separated from each other.

An enlightened being sees the unity in variety and, perceiving the unity of consciousness in the universe, is always in bliss. He either appears to be gazing at the unseen or appears to be submerged in the ocean of consciousness. For others it is very difficult to comprehend his state.

Once when Swamiji was quietly sitting at a lakeside and gazing at the space, someone who was watching him for a long time thought that he was contemplating upon something important.

He asked Swamiji, "What are you thinking about?"

Swamiji replied, "I am not thinking, I am sinking."

"You are sinking? Sinking in what?"

"I am sinking in the Cause."

"Which cause?"

"The cause of this manifestation. The cause of this creation. I am sinking in the cause, which is the cause of all causes. That is pure consciousness. I am sinking in the ocean of consciousness."

The lone reality, the pure consciousness, may appear as many through our external senses and mind but it remains one internally. *In our dreams whatever we see is created by our own consciousness, sustained for some time, and absorbed back in the same consciousness. Similarly, in reality also everything in the universe is created by consciousness, sustained for a specific time cycle and then is absorbed back into the same consciousness.* This is the play of consciousness.

One becomes many and many become One.

As long as the seeker is in search of the sought, the Supreme Divine Being, there is a state of duality. The seeker and the sought are two different entities, but as soon as the seeker finds the sought, then the sought ceases to exist as a separate entity and non-duality is established.

Wherever fire exists, heat and light exist with it, as they are inseparable. Similarly, wherever 'I' exists, know that self also exists, because without the self, 'I' cannot exist as they are both equally inseparable. The divine 'I' of the Supreme Being is the same 'I' in the human being.

Know that we are the divine being in human form. It is not that we as humans are experiencing divinity but it is the divinity which is experiencing human.

The seer, the self, is all-pervasive and is the same in everyone, but the scene which the seer sees is different when seen through different individual beings. His very act of seeing is different in the different individual beings. When this is known then nothing remains unknown. This is the ultimate state of enlightenment.

Nectar of gyana:

- The universe is one block of consciousness. The variety that we perceive in the universe is created by roop maya and naam maya; it is this illusion that is responsible for binding us to the world and entangling us in the cycle of birth, death and rebirth.
- Salvation from the bondage of maya is to see the unity in the variety.
- The perception of non-duality is the ultimate state in spirituality and is the giver of eternal happiness and bliss.
- Learn to dive deep in the ocean of consciousness instead of swimming on its surface. The waves at the surface of the ocean of consciousness will sweep us away from our source.

Object of the Subject

*A*s the seeker started walking, suddenly he saw other seekers, dressed like him in white, walking alongside him.

But this time he was not surprised to see the clear image of himself in all of them as they gradually started increasing in number.

By the time he reached the base of the mountain, he saw hundreds of seekers along with him, each taking a different path to reach the top.

He took a path which was to the left and started his climb. The intensity of the light from the top of the mountain hurt his eyes and made it difficult for him to see the path. Nevertheless, the seeker closed his eyes and started walking on the path guided by his senses. The seamless integration of the senses effortlessly took him to the top. Once he reached the top, he opened his eyes only to find that there was no one around him.

As he went further, at the peak of the mountain he saw the source of the light. The end point, the culmination of his entire journey . . .

In the place of the Buddha there was the seer in an orange *robe.* The seeker was unable to see the face of the seer, blinded as he was by light. But he was awestruck by the mere presence of him. Suddenly realization struck him! A sense of tranquillity prevailed on him as he calmly walked towards the seer. He closed his eyes and stood before him.

After what seems like an eternity, the seer asked the seeker, "O seeker, what have you been seeking?" Without opening his eyes, the seeker said, "I came in search of God, but I only found myself everywhere. And when I searched for myself I only found God. The journey from darkness to light is, in fact, the journey from finite to the infinite."

Swamiji—Sri Poornananda Swamy—and some followers from the ashram went to Karyaar in Tamil Nadu, and my wife and I joined in the group. Close to the hilly region of Karyaar, across a river, in the thick of a jungle, was a place called Banatirtham, where Swamiji had done penance earlier in his life. Some of the followers were excited to visit the same place.

"Don't you want to come with us to see the caves where Swamiji did penance?" asked one of Swamiji's followers.

I shook my head. It seemed foolish to him that we would not join them, and he persisted, "You don't understand the importance of such a place. When we meditate in a place where saints and yogis have meditated, we get the benefit of their vibes present there and be able to experience a heightened state of meditation effortlessly."

"I know that, but I do not know if I will be able to climb up to the caves," I said making an excuse.

I knew beforehand that Swamiji was not going with the group, hence I saw an opportunity to be alone with him, which was otherwise difficult especially with so many people around. I did not want to miss the chance of Swamiji's solitary presence in such a lovely and hilly place like Karyaar.

After everyone left for Banatirtham, we went to see Swamiji. Swamiji was sitting in the veranda of his hut, where he had stayed whenever he visited Karyaar during his penance days. He was all alone.

We went up to him and bowed down in shashtang pranaam.

Swamiji raised his eyebrow as he was surprised to see us.

"Didn't you both go to see the caves of Banatirtham where your guru did penance?" he asked.

"No, Swamiji, we didn't go."

"Why?"

I paused here without any response.

"It is Shivaloka. Don't you have any interest in visiting Shivaloka?" enquired Swamiji further.

Without any hesitation and without a second thought I uttered, "When Shiva himself is here, what is the point in going to Shivaloka, Swamiji?"

Swamiji was surprised to hear this from me. Silent and

obedient, I had never spoken this way till now. Swamiji clapped with a smile.

"Come, sit here near me," said Swamiji, pointing to the ground near his feet.

"The cave is only an object but I am the subject. The subject is the creator of the object. Most of the people get stuck in objects ignoring the importance of the subject," he explained.

Pure consciousness is the cause for manifestation of objects. First, the five elements—ether, air, fire, water, and earth emanated from pure consciousness and, from the various combinations of these elements, emerged various objects and beings.

Objects include all that which can be perceived by the five sense organs. Though objects are nothing but the modified form of subject, yet, because of the limited perceiving capability of the senses and the limited analytical capability of the mind, they appear different, distinct, and separate from the subject.

This perception of everything being different, distinct, and separate from the subject is the main cause of duality and the cause of all suffering in the world. Duality is the main cause for comparison and competition which creates fear, anxiety, enmity, and jealousy. Non-duality liberates us from these negative emotions, thereby establishing the mind in peace.

In an awakened state, whatever we see outside us are the objects as perceived by the five senses. In a dream state, whatever objects we see are not gross objects but objects created by our consciousness and projected on the screen of the mind.

In the Upanishads, it was asked, "What is the reality behind the universe?"

The Upanishads reply, "The underlying reality in the universe is consciousness."

"Who is bound in the world?"

The Upanishad replies, "The consciousness, in the form of beings, is bound."

"How is it bound?"

"Through ignorance."

"Whose ignorance?"

"Its own ignorance. The ignorance of the consciousness itself is the cause for bondage."

Ignorance of the consciousness makes the object feel as though it is a separate entity. Through gyana, contemplation, and meditation on consciousness the ignorance converts back into a state of 'being consciousness'. The self becomes one with the omnipresent, formless consciousness and realizes that it alone exists in the universe. There is no other entity which exists in the universe other than it.

Knowledge of the pure consciousness and its manifesting potential of creation removes the ignorance of duality. It unites everything with the subject and establishes a perfect, enjoyable unity and non-duality in all creation.

NECTAR OF GYANA:

- More than the object, it is the subject which is important. Objects are the perception of the five senses which create duality in the universe.
- Inner perception of the subject, the consciousness, being the underlying reality in the universe creates the unity among all the objects and creates non-duality.
- If you are lucky to find a living guru then do not bother to go to places of worship and places of pilgrimage since the whole universe is contained in the guru. Hence, being in the proximity of the guru gives the same benefit of visiting places of worship and pilgrimages.

Salvation is Right Here, Right Now

S alvation or moksha is generally believed to be a state available after death and not while one is alive. The perception around this is itself flawed. When no one knows what happens after death, then how can one say for sure that salvation or liberation is experienced after death? Instead, liberation has to be experienced before death only.

If salvation is felt and experienced while being alive then one is guaranteed of salvation after death too.

It is to be understood that whatever is our state while we are alive, whatever conditions we impose on the mind, and whatever impressions we imprint on the mind while we are alive will be carried over after death as the post-death state is a continuation of the same life force which animates us in life.

As death is only of the physical body and not of the mind, the mind continues to remain alive based on its conditions, impressions, and feelings even after the death of the body.

Here comes the concept of 'heaven' and 'hell'. The mind experiences heavenly states or tragic states depending on what its nature had been while it was 'alive' within the body. Again, most people have this notion that 'heaven' and 'hell' are two physical places where the physical body stays after death. They also believe that whether one goes to one place or the other depends on the pious or sinful deeds that one does while being alive.

However, in reality, 'heaven' and 'hell' are not physical locations but merely mental states which the mind goes through as a dream after the death of the physical body, depending on the good, bad, scary, or joyful impressions it created while being in the physical body.

So if we feel bound and conditioned to the world, to people and to situations while we are alive then we will remain so even after death. But if we feel liberated from all these bondages then we will continue to remain liberated even after death.

This liberation is experienced when we feel we are neither the physical body, nor the mind, nor the senses, nor the intellect, nor the wisdom, nor the ego of individual existence identified with some name or form, but instead, we identify ourselves with the formless divine 'self'.

If we identify with this 'self' while being alive and witness the activities of the body, mind, ego, and intellect without attributing their actions to ourselves, we enjoy the bliss of liberation.

This state of liberation will continue even after the death of the physical body and we will remain eternally established in the bliss of the Supreme Self, witnessing the universe and its activities without getting attached or engrossed in its functioning or activities.

This is the real state of Liberation, Moksha, and Enlightenment.

The essence of this book is contained in this beautiful song, the 'Poorna Ananda anthem' which we always sing at the end of all our programs.

I am neither the body, nor the senses,
I am neither the mind, nor the wisdom.
Pure consciousness I am, I am the formless . . . Chidananda
roopo Shivoham Shivoham!

I am not in bondage, nor seeking liberation,
I am not in tension, nor in the stress.
Pure consciousness I am, I am the formless . . . Chidananda
roopo Shivoham Shivoham!

I am the creator, I am the creation,
My creation is for my recreation.
Pure consciousness I am, I am the formless . . . Chidananda
roopo Shivoham Shivoham!

Sadguru Rameshji's spiritual journey started under the guidance of Rajendra Brahmachariji, through whose grace he mastered hatha yoga, kundalini yoga, mantra yoga, astral travel, etc., and eventually, by the grace of Swamiji Sri Poornananda, he and his wife Kusum (fondly called Guruma) both attained enlightenment on the same day in the year 1999.

It got revealed in his deep samadhi state as to how the universe manifests from the supreme consciousness, grows, sustains, flourishes and eventually, merges back into its source.

He has dedicated his life to *enlighten* people through regular satsangs and samagams at his ashram. He feels eventually everyone will have to add spiritual flavour in their daily life routine as that alone is the solution for all worldly pains, sufferings, attachments, aversions, stress, happiness, success, prosperity, family harmony, God realization, and self realization.

He has also initiated worldwide campaign *#CleantheCosmos* for a peaceful living among human beings.

Evolve while Involving, Involve while Evolving.
Yad Bhavam, Tad Bhavati.
www.poornaananda.org